A Christian Counselor's Primer On...

For helping those who struggle with.....

Fear & Anxiety

A series of Resource Manuals for Counselors, Pastors, Teachers, Altar Workers, & all those who serve to comfort and equip the Body of Christ.

Book Two

Written by

Debbye Graafsma, bcpc

Awakened!!
Awakened to Grow
Counsel. Classes. Retreats
awakenedtogrow.com

DISCLAIMER

The lesson materials contained in this primer notebook are provided for informational purposes only. These materials, and any or all accompanying materials published by the author, are not in any way intended to diagnose, treat, or evaluate mental illness; nor are they a substitute for professional counseling and care. Those who suffer from the difficulties covered in "A Christian Counselor's Primer On ..." series of booklets should seek additional counsel for their unique situation. Optimally, the materials should be worked through with a trained professional counselor.

The information contained herein is provided for educational purposes only. The user assumes all risks. Debbye Graafsma, and Awakened to Grow, and their affiliates deny responsibility for any and all misuses of the information provided.

Awakened to Grow Ministries
P.O. Box 546
Indian Trail, NC 28079
Website: awakenedtogrow.com

A Christian Counselor's Primer on Fear and Anxiety; A series of resources for those who help others...
Book 2 (ISBN 978-0-9852680-7-7)

©2014 Debbye Graafsma, Awakened to Grow. No portion of this manuscript, nor its accompanying materials may be reproduced or stored by any means or in any format without the written expressed consent of the owners.

A Christian Counselor's Primer on...Fear and Anxiety

Table of Contents

Introduction --- 7

Section One.

    Basic Principles of Growth and Healing-- 9

Section Two.

    Facts about Fear --- 19

Section Three.

    Assessing Sources of Fear -- 35

Section Four.

    The Counselor's Role in Helping Those Who Struggle with Fear-------------- 69

Section Five.

    Required Choices to Heal -- 77

Section Six.

    The Bible on Fear --- 83

Section Seven.

    Scriptural Prayer and Supportive Materials ------------------------------------ 87

Introduction
(Books 1-4)

Dear Fellow Servant,

If you are reading this, you are either considering purchasing this little hand-book or, have already purchased it... Perhaps you are deliberating how you will incorporate it into your ministry or counseling practice. It is my hope that the information contained here will become a tool, to enable and equip you to more effectively hear and Holy Spirit when it comes to helping others. Not only that; but it is my goal to make your efforts even more fruitful, by providing you with Biblical background and lessons to accompany counseling materials.

Each book in this series: "A Christian Counselor's Primer on...." contains current information relevant to its subject, suggested methods of treatment, as well as a series of charts on its topic that I have developed over the past twenty years in private pastoral counseling practice. Over this period of time, I have found my clients respond more positively when I chart out the truths regarding spiritual and emotional conditions. Doing this allows a person to identify their own experience as it relates to the picture presented to them. We then discuss and learn in conversational one-on-one discipling.

Additionally, I have also developed self-assessments and questionnaires for my clients, in order to aid and speed individual discovery. I have included those assessments and/or questionnaires in these hand-books as they relate to the subjects at hand.

At the end of each hand-book are suggested reading lists for you, the counselor, allowing further study, as well as for the client, allowing personal growth and development.

In Christian circles, it is sometimes too easy to give "pat" answers, or "quick fixes," without seeing actual healing and growth take place in the lives of those we are seeking to serve. Such situations render the client feeling inept, or worse, without enough "faith" to find solution. The fact that you are looking at this booklet exempts you from the circles in which those damaging office visits occur. Thank you for your desire to serve: helping and bringing healing to those who are wounded.

That being said, please allow me take a couple of moments to encourage you.

The ministry of providing a safe place for counsel is a vital one. So much brokenness exists in our society today; so much pain. And yet, only one person out of every four people who are referred to a counseling office will actually make the call and follow-through to keep the appointment. And, of those in that 25 percentile, only around half will actually commit to applying the training they receive in sessions, realizing change and growth. That means that together, as counselors, all of us have about a 13% chance of helping anyone! Believe it or not, that is really good news! After all, just one transformed life can change the world!!

Imagine. What could happen if thirteen out of every one hundred people in your sphere of influence became impassioned and empowered to grow, not only emotionally, but spiritually as well?

Years ago, General Motors' famed inventor and head of research, Charles Kettering, made a very wise declaration in describing how his department approached the concept of designing need-meeting vehicles. He said, "A problem well-defined is half-solved." Not only is this statement true when it comes to designing cars, but it is also true when it comes to the process of learning to choose well in living.

When a client can see the "why" of their struggle in growth and healing, they are more than half-way to discovering the repentant heart and desire to change they need to acquire more healing and therefore, health in their Christian Walk! An encounter with God is then just steps away! Hopefully, using the materials contained here will make than encounter a reality!

In the beginning of each volume, I explain a little about how the Father God's principles of healing work when it comes to emotional healing and spiritual development; with each volume building on the prior volume's teaching. Hopefully, this will help you to discover a sense of empowerment and personal mission. After all, that's why each of us began in this helping ministry......

It is my hope to help you and bless you!

Blessings!

Debbye Graafsma, M.Div., D.Min., bcpc
Awakened to Grow Ministries

Section One
Basic Principles of Growth and Healing
(for Books 1-4; Jesus' parable, "The Sower and the Soil")

There are twelve volumes in the "A Christian Counselor's Primer on…." series of handbooks. Within each volume are five manuals, or "quick-study" texts, designed to provide an overview of the materials presented. For Books 1-4, we will consider the first parable Jesus Christ told during His ministry on earth: "The Sower and the Soil" as a springboard for basic understanding.

There is such hope and encouragement to be drawn from this parable. And the fact that it was the first parable Jesus told, also gives us a glimpse of the attitude of Abba Father towards us – even when we are in the worst of conditions.

The idea of healing the hearts of men and women began with Jesus. Continually, throughout His ministry on earth, our God spoke to the very roots and cause of the Pain and dysfunction each of us carry: our baggage, if you will. It is His method to say, "You have heard it said – but *I say to you….*" And then He finishes the statement with something that changes the entire perspective on whatever subject He was speaking.

Jesus came to heal. Jesus came to restore. Jesus came to redeem and rebuild those things lost and broken; those parts of us deemed as beyond repair.

The parable of the Sower is particularly precious in my own life, because the Holy Spirit used it in my own life to challenge my personal depth meter when it comes to emotional and spiritual development.

And let me just say this as we begin: Spiritual development and Emotional maturity cannot be separated. It is impossible to become a healthy, emotionally congruent individual, without finding ourselves at a crossroads of sorts. What will I do with the spiritual issues that stir in my soul when I decide I want to experience "more?" What answers will I allow to pervade and influence my mind and heart? By the same token, personal spiritual development cannot become a reality, unless I choose to yield yet again to the Holy Spirit of the Living God, and allow Him to challenge, confront, and change the attitudes and patterns of my dysfunctional past; allow Him to mold and form on deeper and deeper core levels, His nature and Personality within me….

Jesus Christ was a master Storyteller. In imparting Life-truths, He would weave a story that people related to and were fascinated by. The Sower and the Soil is one of my favorites. Jesus explained this particular parable as being about the human heart; or what we would describe the soul. *(The human soul, is comprised of our mind, will and emotions; what we think, choose and feel.)*

Before we go to the parable, let me share a couple of charts with you, that I hope will serve you well in your desire to help others. When I first began counseling, these were some of the first I developed, and I find I use each of them at least once a day, even now.

The first chart, is the description of the Levels of Relationship and Communication. This is a basic chart that defines the difference between IQ, Intelligence Quotient, and EQ, Emotional Quotient. Emotional Quotient, or Emotional Intelligence, as it is being referred to these days, has to do with one's ability to relate to other people. EQ has to do with the deeper levels of living we all experience with the people we are closest to in relationships.

Jesus referred to the Emotional Quotient, as the "Heart of Man."

Please consider the IQ/EQ chart below.

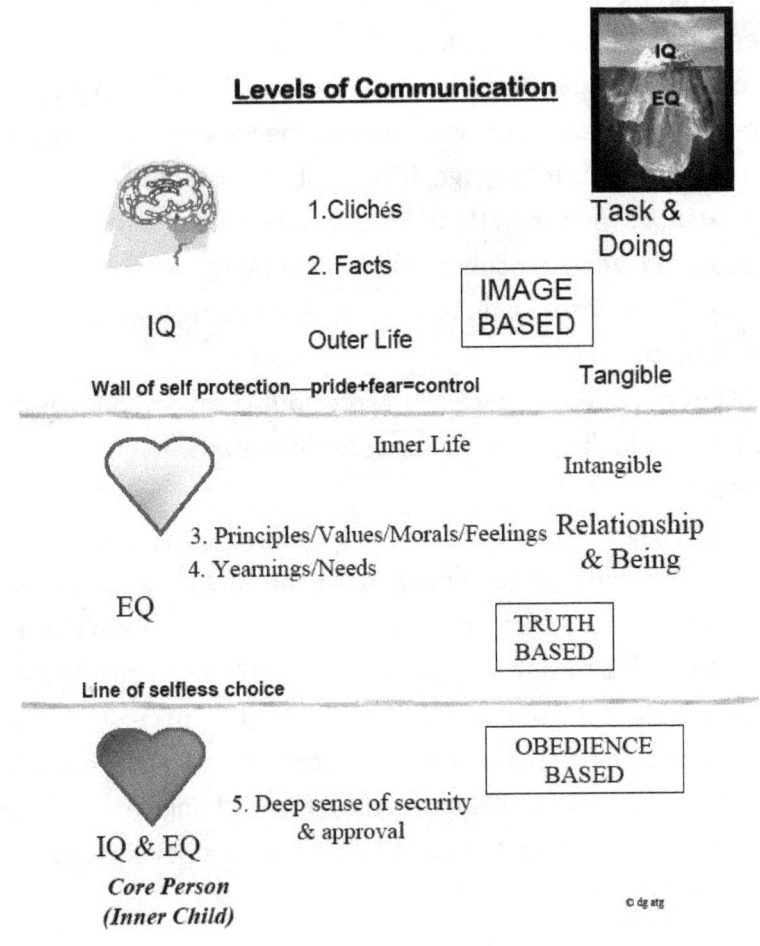

When we study this chart, we discover the differing depths of relationship each of us experience in our lives.

Level 1 = Clichés — These are the people we meet once on an elevator, or in a crowded room, and make **surface-level conversation** with, experiencing no fear or sense of risk.

Level 2 = Facts — These are the relationships we encounter in our lives who require **a little more expenditure from us – but still without emotional impartation.** For example, when we are in school, we must memorize and repeat the facts. How well we remember many of the facts determines our Intelligence Quotient. (That is, "are we intelligent, able to apply the facts?" Also, "how well do our life achievements 'stack up' against others' lives, etc.")

A life lived on only levels 1 and 2 will be image based, success oriented, shallow in nature, and dependent upon performance orientation.

Between levels 2 and 3, there exists a Wall of Self-Protection. The wall is comprised of Pride and/or Fear. Simply put, Fear + Pride = Control. Most of us construct our personal wall in pre-puberty, or just after, depending upon the comparisons we make between our "nest" and the "nests" of those in our friendship circle, and how our own sense of "normal" compares to the "normal" of our friends and acquaintances.

Level 3 = A *man* will experience Level 3 of relationships when he is able to determine his personal **principles and values**, and express them to his companions. A *woman* will experience Level 3 in relationships when she is able to express her **morals and feelings** to her companions. There are reasons for these differences in approaching this level of relationship differently; gender being the main reason.

Level 4 = **Yearnings and needs** are what make up the deepest part of our being. In this level, we are able to share our hopes and dreams as they relate to our future. These are the deepest perceived needs we carry; many times without expression.

A life lived incorporating levels 3 and 4 into daily experience, will manifest the Personhood of a well-bonded individual. Such a person has chosen to cease trying to "hold to the image" of who he or she believes must be portrayed in day to day living.

However, what actually fuels, or gives power to, the Emotional Quotient levels of our lives is the substance of Truth. In places where we have learned to believe our experiences as being the source of Truth, we will develop broken trust and an inability to relate to others in a healthy way. (This is something we all do.)

When we become believers in Christ, the Holy Spirit begins the process of personal transformation; bringing comfort, healing, change and growth. In the midst of this maturation, there comes a point in the life of every believer when he or she is confronted with the realization of the disparities and contrasts between what our experiences and taught us to be true, and the Truth of God's Word.

If a person chooses to cling to the perceptions he or she has always believed; the person's own conclusions of "truth;" then the processes of emotional development and spiritual maturation cease. Sadly, when this type of refusal to the Spirit's formation occurs, any future discoveries the believer receives will be tainted by that refusal; influenced by elements of fear and legalism.

In contrast, when a believer is willing to take the risk of trusting God for their emotional development, the Holy Spirit (the Helper and Teacher) continues the process of healthy emotional and spiritual development by breathing courage into the soul. He then will confront the believer with the need to exchange those inward perceptions of "truth" for Abba Father's Truth. When our "truth," or perception, is traded for God the Father's Truth, the Bible becomes a template learning how to live the life of a believer. At that point of growth, the Word of God becomes real to us; more than mental assent.

At that point, *His Truth* becomes voluntarily traded for *our truth*. *His Truth* is durable, unshakable, and trustworthy.

Then, as we continue our lives in Jesus Christ, at some future point of our development, we each must come to another place of choosing. This second choice presents us with as question. Will we allow the Holy Spirit to deepen our resolve and obedience with God?

This is the choice to move forward without looking back. It is at this point we discover that we are disciples of Jesus Christ. This second choice, or "wall," if you will, is the fear which confronts us when we seek to give our lives away, or invest our efforts into a cause that will benefit others. When the choice towards discipleship is make, we become willing to offer something of ourselves to God, and to others, simply for the common good. We do it with a sense of purpose and fulfillment, and it is an offering that comes from deep within.

This deepest part of us, I refer to as the Core, or Inner Child.

Now, let's take a look at how those levels of communication affect our personal relationships.

The journey of the Christian life is one that takes us inward, as well as one that focuses our intentions outward. The inward journey of personal Discovery and Empowerment requires the confronting of imprinting, pain and experiences with cause us to be malformed in our emotional growth and development. This is what only the Creator can re-imprint and heal. After all, God is the only Perfect Parent. The outward journey determines the direction of our personal development. It also maintains our balance. In this journey, the Holy Spirit teaches us how to express His care and love for others – without pretense or fear, as disciples of the Living God.

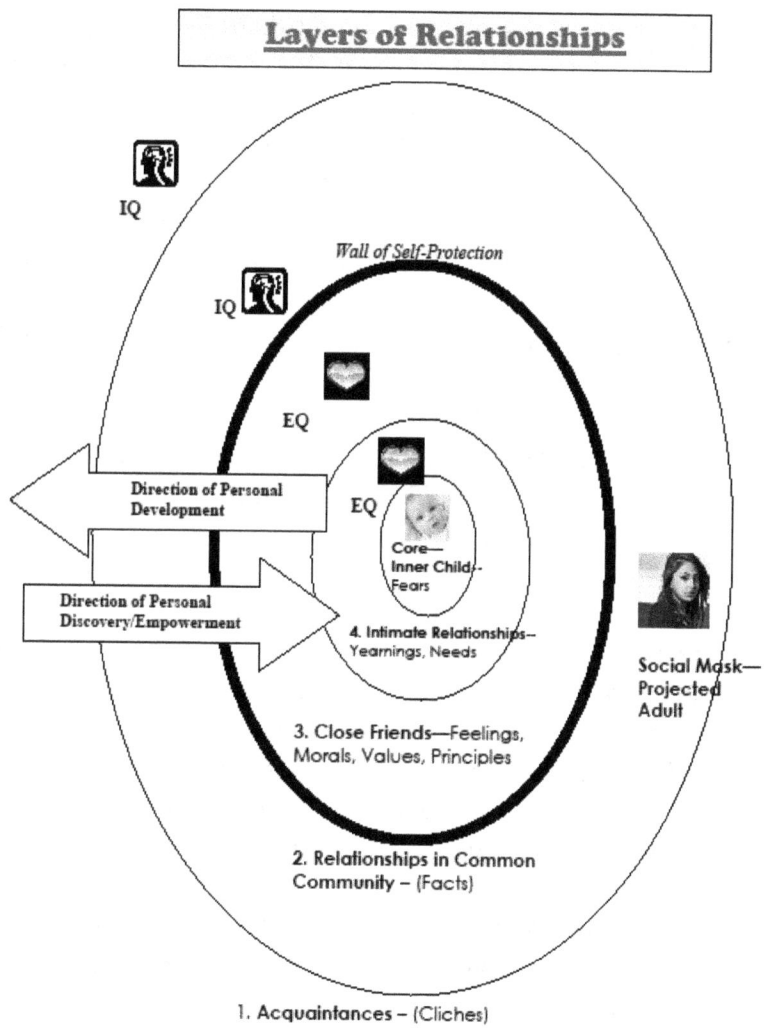

Jesus continually referred to this growth and discovery process. In Matthew 13, our Savior told a parable about a sower, his seed, and the soil.

> "That day Jesus went out of the house and was sitting by the sea. And large crowds gathered to Him, so He got into a boat and sat down, and the whole crowd was standing on the beach. And He spoke many things to them in parables, saying, "Behold, the sower went out to sow; and as he sowed, some seeds fell beside the road, and the birds came and ate them up. Others fell on the rocky places, where they did not have much soil; and immediately they sprang up, because they had no depth of soil. But when the sun had risen, they were scorched; and because they had no root, they withered away. Others fell among the thorns, and the thorns came up and choked them out. And others fell on the good soil and yielded a crop, some a hundredfold, some sixty, and some thirty. He who has ears, let him hear.
>
> And the disciples came and said to Him, "Why do You speak to them in parables?" Jesus answered them, "To you it has been granted to know the mysteries of the kingdom of heaven, but to them it has not been granted. For whoever has, to him more shall be given, and he will have an abundance; but whoever does not have, even what he has shall be taken away from him. Therefore I speak to them in parables; because while seeing they do not see, and while hearing they do not hear, nor do they understand. In their case the prophecy of Isaiah is being fulfilled, which says, YOU WILL KEEP ON HEARING, BUT WILL NOT UNDERSTAND; YOU WILL KEEP ON SEEING, BUT WILL NOT PERCEIVE; FOR THE HEART OF THIS PEOPLE HAS BECOME DULL, WITH THEIR EARS THEY SCARCELY HEAR, AND THEY HAVE CLOSED THEIR EYES, OTHERWISE THEY WOULD SEE WITH THEIR EYES, HEAR WITH THEIR EARS, AND UNDERSTAND WITH THEIR HEART AND RETURN, AND I WOULD HEAL THEM.'
>
> But blessed are your eyes, because they see; and your ears, because they hear. For truly I say to you that many prophets and righteous men desired to see what you see, and did not see it, and to hear what you hear, and did not hear it. Hear then the parable of the sower. When anyone hears the word of the kingdom and does not understand it, the evil one comes and snatches away what has been sown in his heart. This is the one on whom seed was sown beside the road. The one on whom seed was sown on the rocky places, this is the man who hears the word and immediately receives it with joy; yet he has no firm root in himself, but is only temporary, and when affliction or persecution arises because of the word, immediately he falls away. And the one on whom seed was sown among the thorns, this is the man who hears the word, and the worry of the world and the deceitfulness of wealth choke the word, and it becomes unfruitful. And the one on whom seed was sown on the good soil, this is the man who hears the word and understands it; who indeed bears fruit and brings forth, some a hundredfold, some sixty, and some thirty."

In this parable, Jesus speaks of four different levels of soil. He likens each level of soil to a condition of a person's soul. As you read, consider and remember the four levels of communication, and the four levels of relationship.

1. Trampled, hardened – describing the soul of a person who does not understand Kingdom life, and who dismisses the Word as not being necessary for living.

2. Rocky, shallow – describing the soul of a person who has many hard and stony places in their heart. They can hear the Truth and have a desire to learn, until they are corrected or confronted. They lack the ability to follow through, and things outside the Presence of God gain attention and loyalty.

3. Weedy, thorny – describing the soul of a person who has battles with distraction in their desire to walk a solid walk with Jesus.

4. Good soil – 30, 60 and 100 fold – describing the soul of a person who receives the seed of God's Truth with an open heart and responds with obedience and teachability. Notice that good soil has degrees of fruitfulness.

In this parable, Jesus refers to these differing qualities of soil as being descriptive of the state of the heart of man. This was the first parable Jesus told in His ministry on earth; which makes it highly significant in looking at how God views the condition of our soul when it comes to our ability to relate to Him and to Truth. For me personally, it reminds me that Abba Father made man and woman in His image, placing them in the Garden of Eden to cultivate it and keep it. That would mean that our God has always been a cultivator; a Gardener of the soul, if you will.

What is most encouraging about this parable is that soil quality can be changed. Just like a physical garden, hard work is involved to break up the hard soil, remove the stones, and weeds. And, just like a physical garden, fertilizer is added to soften and enrich the soil. In relational terms, the "fertilizer" which enriches the soil of the heart of man, would be the life lessons (God-given) we take away from the painful experiences in our lives.

As we walk through the first five books in the primer series, please remember the levels of soil, and how they relate to the levels of communication and relationships. Over the past twenty years, I have used these comparisons in the ministry of pastoral counseling; seeing results in the lives of believers as well as disciples.

The four types of soil Jesus referred to in the Sower's parable, directly relate to the four levels of communication and relationship, listed and shown below.

IQ	1. Clichés 2. Facts	*Image based – intelligence* *Task and Doing oriented*
EQ	3. Values, Principles (male) Morals, Feelings (female) 4. Yearnings and Needs	*Truth based – heart of man* *Relationship and Be-ing oriented*
Core	**Inner Child**	*Real self/spiritual perceptions* *Obedience and Inner Approval oriented*

There are many areas of relational living which correspond to these four levels of relationship. For a more detailed addressing of this subject, and to pinpoint a person's placement in growth, please consider utilizing the G.E.M.S. Personal Assessment Tool, (Section M), by Debbye Graafsma. *(Available through Awakened to Grow, or online.)*

When a person lives in a healthy state, individual Personhood is expressed through the whole being. This is called Congruency. On a practical level, the person portrays the same personality in all settings of living. They are strong enough in their Core to withstand the pressures and intimidations of varying environments.

When we come to Christ, becoming believers for the first time, very rarely is anyone congruent. That process begins when we choose to yield to the Spirit of God, allowing Him access and permission to shape us into the likeness of Christ.

In considering these truths, I have provided a chart on the next page, which combines the work of cultivation or gardening, with the condition of the soil on each level. It is my hope it will encourage you as you encounter believers as well as disciples in your ministry as a helper/counselor.

The Sower and the Seed: Becoming A Cultivated & Well Watered Garden

"The Lord will guide you continually, and satisfy your soul in drought, and strengthen your bones, and you shall be like a watered garden, and like a spring of water, whose waters do not fail." Isaiah 58:11

The Parable: Matthew 13:3-9 and 18-23

Type of Soil Vs 3-9	Jesus' Meaning vs 18-23	Condition of the Heart	A Gardener's Solution	Spiritual Application
1. Seed on the wayside -- was devoured by birds	Not understood. Devil steals it. Survivor mentality	Numb, Trodden down By reason of conditioning has become rock hard feels used.	Soak with water. Break up crusty earth. Dig deep earth. Dig. Remove rocks. Add fertilizer and conditioners before planting. Feed well.	Has learned to believe a lie Life experiences have wounded and closed the heart. (emotionally and spiritually)
2. Seed on stony places -- no depth, withered by elements	Receives, but has No depth in himself to make application, is offended by difficulty and falls away only. No joy. "Tell me what the rules are – I'll do that."	Unaware of deeper possibilities. Too many hard things with no understanding or ability to resolve. Functioning plants well.	Water well to loosen earth. Remove stones. Dig down to rock. Add fertilizer and conditioners. Feed	Sees the stones. Feel stuck. Difficulties argue with the love of God. The heart wants to trust, but fears repetition of pain. (trusts self most)
3. Seed among thorns -- new growth crowded by weeds	Receives, but has so many other things "going on right now" any application is squeezed out, becomes unfruitful	Aware of deeper growth Drawn by Holy Spirit -- is easily distracted by obligations and responsibilities. Content to maintain on surface but lives unfulfilled	Weed out crowded growth beds. Spade around plants for aerating soil. Add fertilizer. Condition soil. Water well. Monitor for sprouts of weed seeds not pulled on first try.	Is weed aware, assumes they are normal – is used to emotional clutter. Fearful of Change – task oriented for security. (works based. Condemnation focused, fear driven)
4. Seed on good ground -- yielded a crop	Receives, understands, allows it to grow, and bears life- fruit	Open and vulnerable Teachable, receiving truth and making application personal changes daily indicate growth	Maintain weed free status. Maintain condition of soil. Regular cultivation and aeration for health. New plantings and pruning as applicable.	Maturity takes time, growth takes time. There are no substitutes. Discipleship involves discovery. Emotional health and spiritual maturity cannot be separated. Daily maintenance will ensure continued development.

Section Two
Facts about Fear

"What Does Fear Look Like?"
"How Can I See it Coming?"

"The oldest and strongest emotion of mankind is fear."
H.P. Lovecraft

Fear is a broad subject, overshadowing a plethora of emotional territory. In the counseling field, it has come to serve as the basis for many issues and diagnoses, from worry and anxiety, to full blown panic attacks and behavioral disorders. In fact, Fear is usually referred to as a primal emotion, meaning its existence is part of man's original nature.

Within Christianity, confusion exists in some circles regarding Fear. In Christian counseling, Fear is recognized as not only an emotional issues, but as a spiritual one as well. This handbook deals with the *emotional* symptoms and effects of Fear. For a more indepth discussion of the *spiritual* implications and effects of the spirit of Fear, please refer to our workbook, "The Caleb Principle: Life-long Liberation." (For a thorough addressing of both types of Fear, it is a good idea to utilize both workbooks.)

In human terms, Fear is described as:

> *"An unpleasant emotion caused by the belief that someone or something is dangerous, likely to cause pain, or a threat. Also described as terror, fright, fearfulness, horror, alarm, panic, agitation, trepidation, dread, consternation, dismay, and/or distress."*
> (Source: The Oxford Dictionary)

We see the results of Fear's presence in our culture, as well as within our lives. For example:

- 65 million people suffer with high blood pressure
- 1 million people die of heart disease
- Millions of people are afflicted with ulcers and stomach problems
- Millions of people have panic/anxiety disorder. (#1 for women, #2 for men)
- 40-50 million people deal with a sleep disorder of some kind
- 80 million people deal with headaches
- Millions of people deal with depression.

Millions of people deal with phobias, and obsessive/compulsive disorders.

Surprisingly, Fear can cause somatic symptoms (physical) in the body, as a person tries to inwardly process their emotions, seeking normalcy. Some of those symptoms can and may include:

Heart palpitations	Headaches	Shortness of breath
Perspiration	Racing thoughts	A desire to just "leave"
Inward shakiness	Dizziness	Difficulty breathing
Faintness	Chest pain	Gastric cramps
Diarrhea/frequent urination	Fatigue	Sexual problems
Fibromyalgia	Sleep difficulties	Decreased concentration
Nightmares	Emotional sensitivity	Allergic reactions
Ezcema outbreaks	Skin eruptions	Immunity disorders
Krohn's disease	Weight Gain	Weight Loss

Did you know?

> ***One of the most effective antidotes for stress and anxiety is the right amount of sleep: (8.5-9 hours per night).***

**Fear is recognized with different labels in varying degrees of intensity.
Please see the chart below, "Evidences of Fear."**

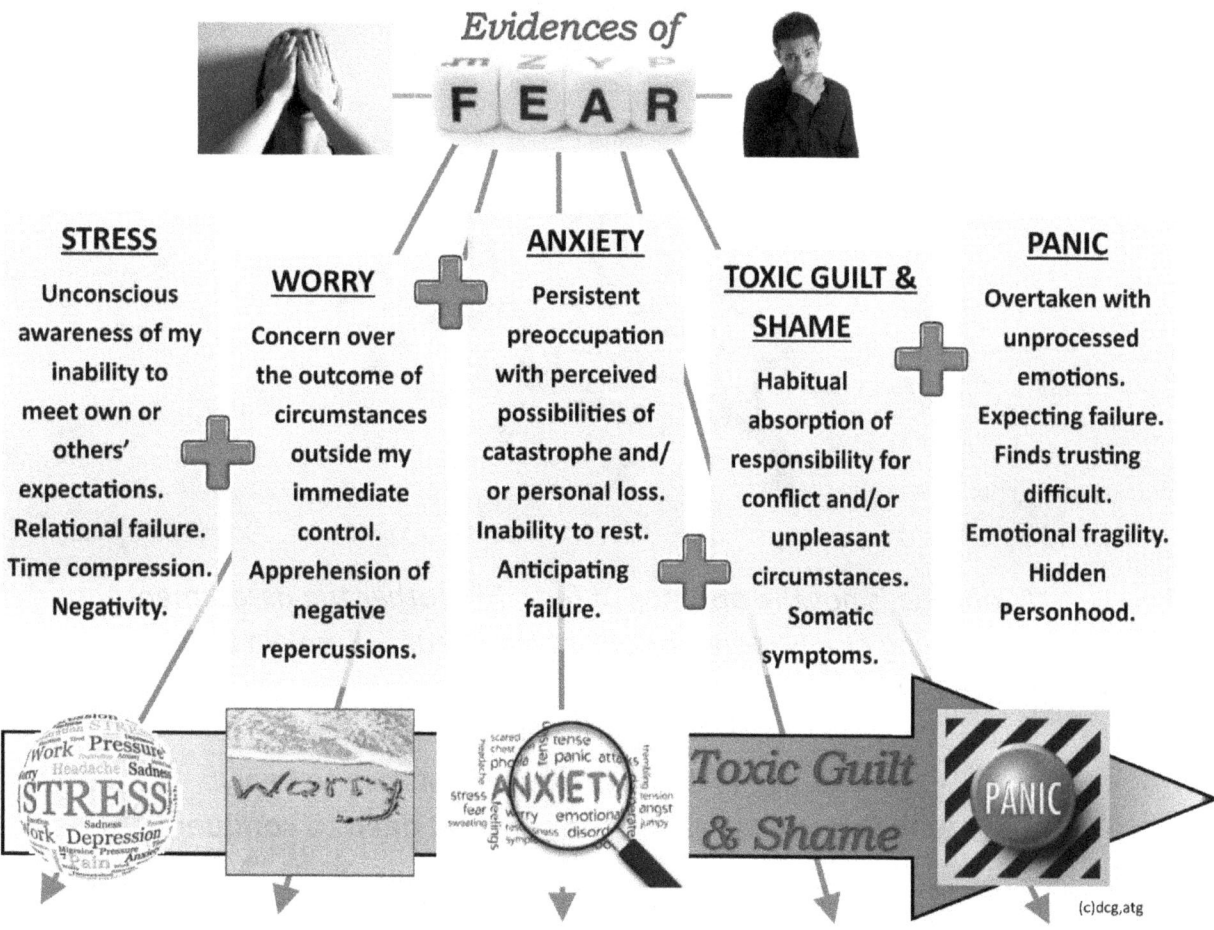

The intensity of a client's presentation will depend upon several determinations:

1. The depth of the trauma/relationship which invoked the fear.
2. The length of time since the choice was made to acquiesce to fear.
3. The degree of health in day-to-day personal coping mechanisms.
4. Emotional health in other areas of living.
5. The amount of intentionality/readiness possessed to move forward.

"Courage is not the absence of fear, but rather the assessment that something else is more important than fear." Franklin D. Roosevelt

**In other words,
Courage is the conscious resistance to Fear,
with the awareness of our personal need to conquer it.**

Forms of Fear
Stress, Worry, Anxiety, Toxic Shame/Guilt, Panic

Many times, the medical community refers to "fear" as "anxiety." What is anxiety?

Every person on the planet has experienced the feeling of worry, or even anxiousness when approaching a new situation or relationship. Have you ever felt your throat go tight just before you were about to give a speech, or go through a job interview?

Instances of mild insecurity, or nervousness can often cause us to experience forms of Fear. Sometimes, our response to Fear is to absorb it, allowing ourselves to become stressed. Sometimes those experiences can work to our advantage, making us more alert and aware. Surprisingly, there are some people who find they are better thinkers in emergency situations when they are just a "little afraid."

In fact, our western world has become so accustomed to living in a state of stress, we have learned to habitually maintain it, even to the point of overscheduling our lives and the lives of our children. In his book **Life's Hidden Addictions**, Dr. Archibald Hart refers to this lifestyle as "Adrenaline Addiction." According to Hart, our culture has learned to crave doses of unhealthy amounts of caffeine and "energy producing" substances, trying to normalize and satisfy our stress patterns.

Additionally, our normalized patterns of stressful living are then reinforced and passed down both culturally and generationally. When life-patterns and traditional expectations come into conflict with our human limitations, we tend to fall into the trap of expecting ourselves to practice "stress management" rather than a healthy lifestyles. In so doing, we have learned to tolerate entry levels of Fear as necessary for survival.

When a person lives in these patterns over long periods, with unconscious levels of stress and anxiety normalized, the ability to function on a day-to-day basis is greatly challenged. Eventually, coping skills no longer suffice. This is the state in which most clients who present with fear arrive in the counseling office.

It is a good idea for a counselor to have a general understanding of Fear based disorders and how they might show themselves in the clients you encounter.

Anxiety Disorders

Note: All human beings experience normal levels of anxiety; usually in anticipation of a new experience, a challenging relationship or situation, or upcoming responsibility. Sometimes, a short period of minimal fear will occur in such cases. The symptoms of normal anxiety include slightly elevated blood pressure, increased perspiration, shortness of breath, need to urinate, or minimal nausea.

A disorder, however, occurs repeatedly, and a person's physical symptoms are much more pronounced. If a client presents without being medicated, it is wise to refer the person to their own medical doctor for medication while they are in the midst of processing the reason for the disorder's occurrence.

Anxiety Related Disorders. A related disorder involves an intense fear, usually in regard to specific things or circumstances. Specific anxieties could indicate specific animals (like a black cat), or circumstance (like being trapped in a small space). Social fears have to do with group environments are public situations.

Generalized Anxiety Disorders. A generalized anxiety disorder shows itself with recurring worries and/or fears. A person might be tormented with worries about finances, or health. Many times, such a person will feel a "dark cloud" hanging over them; a sense that a terrible event is looming just ahead in the future. This person will have a difficult time identifying the source of their fears. Such a disorder can interfere with the completion of daily responsibilities and tasks.

Panic Disorders. This disorder shows itself in unexpected, forceful and unreasonable emotions of trepidation and alarm. Sadly, daily life many times becomes constricted for individuals with this disorder. There is a pervading sense of doom when it comes to stepping into public situations, or unknown/new environments. The fear of embarrassment from an additional attack prevents the ability to relax, rest or enjoy life and its activities.

Panic attacks are not life-threatening, but involve symptoms, such as a pounding heartbeat, shortness of breath, and the feeling of losing control, or fear of dying. Usually 5 to 20 minutes long, a panic attack may be triggered by stressful circumstances, and can occur unexpectedly. The body's automatic "fight or flight" response is triggered, and prepares a person to run away from danger, even when it is not needed at all. The body reacts to these triggers as if a person is facing a life threatening situation, even though they may not be in danger at all. The result if alarming physical symptoms, and emotions.

A panic disorder is diagnosed when a person has repeated panic attacks, or when they worry intensely about having another attack, and avoid places and events where they anticipate another attack could occur. A panic disorder is indicated when a person changes their lifestyle to accommodate their fears of having another attack. However, having a panic attack does not automatically mean a person has a disorder. Panic attacks can occur with other anxiety disorders as well.

Exact causes are still not clear, but several factors may be responsible: an imbalance of brain chemicals (neuro-transmitters), a family history of panic attacks, faulty thinking methods and wrong life approach systems, poorly managed stress, and unresolved psychological issues (past pain).

Triggers have been found to include: certain medications (specifically asthma and heart condition meds), too much nicotine or caffeine in the body, alcohol abuse, drug usage (specifically methamphetamines, marijuana, cocaine, LSD), and overactive thyroid.

Feelings of intense fear, terror, anxiety, accompanied with difficulty breathing, or rapid breathing (hyperventilation), chest pain or tightness, a racing or irregular heartbeat, dizziness, sweating, shaking. Some report episodes of sleep paralysis (unable to move during sleep), or nervous shaking (in Hispanic cultures, "ataque de nervios").

Half of persons (50%) who experience panic attacks, also deal with agoraphobia (the fear and avoidance of public places and situations). Panic disorder and depression also frequently occur together. Substance abuse is also a symptom of panic disorder in a majority of cases.

Obsessive Compulsive Disorder. This disorder displays unwelcome, overwhelming and insistent emotions and thinking patterns (obsessions and rituals). These thinking patterns are often accompanied by inner compulsions which the person feels must be satisfied in order to maintain a sense of safety. A person suffering from this condition might turn a light switch on and off five times each time they enter a room, or fastidiously clean because of germs, or wash hands excessively. They never are satisfied with their own efforts, and tend to be extremely detail oriented.

Post-Traumatic Stress Disorder. Commonly referred to as PTSD, this disorder usually occurs when a person has experienced trauma (such as a witnessing a crime, a natural disaster, or experiencing a personal violation). Activities, patterns of thinking, emotions and relationships become seriously affected. Anything can serve as a reminder of the trauma; a color, a similar situation, even an odor. Such reminders trigger an inner re-experiencing of the incident, and be accompanied by a wave of deep depression, rage, or a panic attack.

Symptoms include repeated, vivid, distressing memories, flashbacks, or dreams of the traumatic events; avoiding situations that remind you of the event, not being able to recall or discuss parts of the event. People who deal with this disorder can become emotionally numb, detached, or uninterested in important activities. They also deal with feeling keyed-up, irritable, or easily startled. These persons have difficulty sleeping and/or concentrating. There is also a pervading sense of fearing for personal safety, or feeling like they will not live a long life for no apparent reason. These and other similar symptoms can disrupt and disable work and relationships. These symptoms can develop as soon as one month after a traumatic event, although some symptoms may not develop until years later. Half of all people with this disorder experience the symptoms for three months or more.

PTSD can linger for years after an event. Examples would include veterans returning from active warfare, adults who experienced sexual abuse/rape as children, those who have witnessed bloodshed, those who have been exposed to or threatened with violence, to name a few.

This disorder affects 8-10% of the population. An additional 5-15% of people may have symptoms without developing a full-scale disorder. A traumatic event is one in which a person experiences intense feelings of fear, helplessness, and/or horror. Many times, persons with this disorder develop substance abuse issues in addition to the anxiety.

PTSD can occur in children, who will show additional symptoms to those listed above, commonly with behavioral problems, or even repeatedly acting out the event. When the symptoms occur immediately following a crises, the disorder is labelled, "acute stress disorder," and symptoms will last for close to a month.

A family with a history of depression, abuse, or trauma has a greater risk of developing this disorder. Women are twice as likely as men to succumb to PTSD, in most cases because they tend to be more subjective in life approach.

Prejudices. A pre-disposition of distrust toward other people, hindering community and honest relationship, based upon stereo-types and assumptions. Such stereo-types usually have to do with people groups, such as race, religion, status, social class, or gender. The predisposition to prejudice sets the stage for distrust, and then that distrust opens the door to full-blown fears, then phobias.

Distrust. A period of warning before actual fear begins, sometimes explained as an inward feeling of caution, usually focused towards a person, a situation or an object.

Distrust is a lack of faith or belief, described as a warning feeling towards something questionable or unknown. For example, having distrust of a rickety old bridge across a 100 ft. drop.

Nightmares and Night Terrors. A nightmare can be defined as a bad dream, from which a person can be awakened fully, and usually can remember with fairly good clarity. A night terror differs from a nightmare in the sense that it occurs when the person is experiencing the deepest levels of non- REM sleep. Even if awakened, the person rarely can remember the episode, except for a deep sense of panic. When the subject is roused, they are not fully awake, even when efforts are made to awaken the sleeper. A night terror can occur for 10-20 minutes at a time, and the sleeper could even have open eyed communication and remain asleep. While each night terror will be different, all episodes of the same person will generally have similar traits. One universal quality of night terros is a strong sense of danger. Usually there is a being, tangible or otherwise, who wishes to hurt the sleeping person.

Many sufferers of night terrors are reluctant to speak of them because of their violent, graphic and disturbing nature. About 3% of children ages 4-6 experience night terrors, and episodes can occur for 2-3 weeks at a time, and then go away. There are a multitude of triggers, but emotional stress during the previous day, and a high fever is thought to precipitate most episodes. The best method of combatting sleep terrors is to ensure the person maintains a consistent and healthy sleep schedule.

Social Anxiety Disorder. Also called "social phobia," Social Anxiety Disorder is a psychological condition causing an overwhelming fear of social situations that require interacting with or performing in front of others. It is different from being shy, introverted, or experiencing normal anxiety before public speaking. The person is afraid they will somehow become embarrassed or will embarrass others with what you say or do in public. Social anxiety disorder causes relentless fear, often beginning days or weeks before an event. Often, the disorder triggers physical symptoms such as blushing, sweating, shakiness, rapid heartbeat, and difficulty concentrating. This disorder significantly impacts a person's daily life, and can cause withdrawal from social activities, work and/or school.

The exact cause of this disorder is not known; whether it is a genetic pre-disposition, running in families, or if it is a learned response developed after experiencing a particularly humiliating situation, or whether both catalysts could be to blame.

Social anxiety disorder has emotional and physical symptoms. Emotionally, the symptoms are feelings of anxiety, sadness, and being easily startled in anticipation of an event. Excessive worry or fearing that something bad will happen at that event. As a result of these emotions, some have been known to become nauseous and become ill.

Additionally, persons with social anxiety disorder often struggle with substance abuse, or other addictions.

Paranoia. A psychosis (a belief system, stemming from a short-circuit in brain connection), relating to a false perception of being persecuted. This perception often cases one to change their normal behavior in radical ways. After a time, their behavior may become extremely compulsive.

Terror. A pronounced state of fear, which usually occurs after the state of horror, when someone becomes overwhelmed with a sense of immediate danger. Thus, terror overwhelms the person to the point of making irrational choices and non-typical behavior.

Neurotic Anxiety. Hot sweats, things go blank in the brain, exaggerated feelings of helplessness, a sense of dread in the midst of mild or even non-existent danger.

Anxiety disorders can also be brought about by side effects or withdrawal from certain drugs. Such drugs include caffeine, alcohol, nicotine, cold remedies, decongestants, bronchodilators for asthma, tricyclic anti-depresssants, cocaine, amphetamines, diet pills, ADHD medications and thyroid medications.

~~~

A poor diet can also contribute to stress or anxiety – for example, low levels of vitamin B complex, especially B-12.

~~~

In very rare cases, a tumor of the adrenal gland could be the cause of anxiety. The symptoms in that case are caused by an overproduction of hormones reponsible for the feelings of anxiety.

The Brain's Involvement with Fear Response

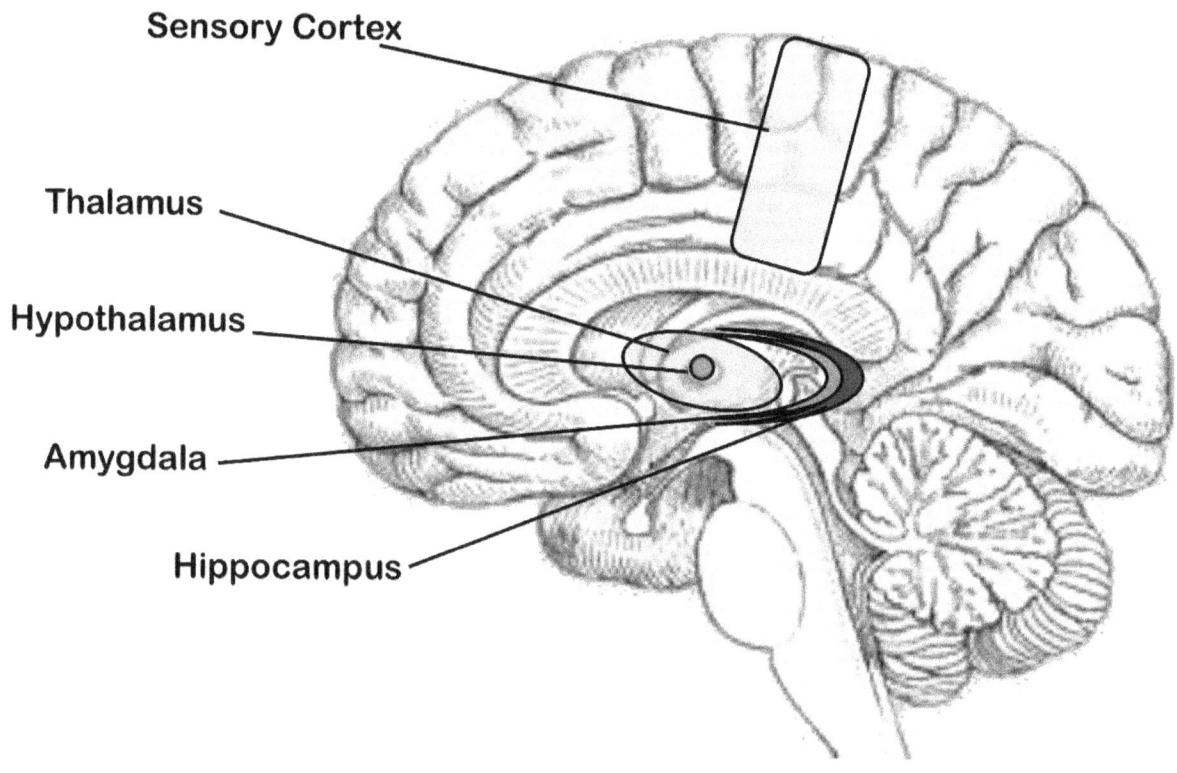

Somatic Conspiracies that Complicate Anxiety.

Hypothalmus and Pituitary Glands. The glands within the human body that regulate blood pressure, heart rate, body temperature, sleep patterns, hunger and thirst. When stress or anxiety are present, these go into over-drive.

Adrenal Glands. The glands within the human body which work with the thyroid to regulate energy levels, metabolism, structure of hair, skin tone etc. When stress and anxiety are present, these glands pump into the body, raising heart rate and blood pressure. Without healthy adrenaline management, the body absorbs this excess adrenaline, and begins the process of stress related diseases.

Somatic Responses to Stress, Anxiety and Anger

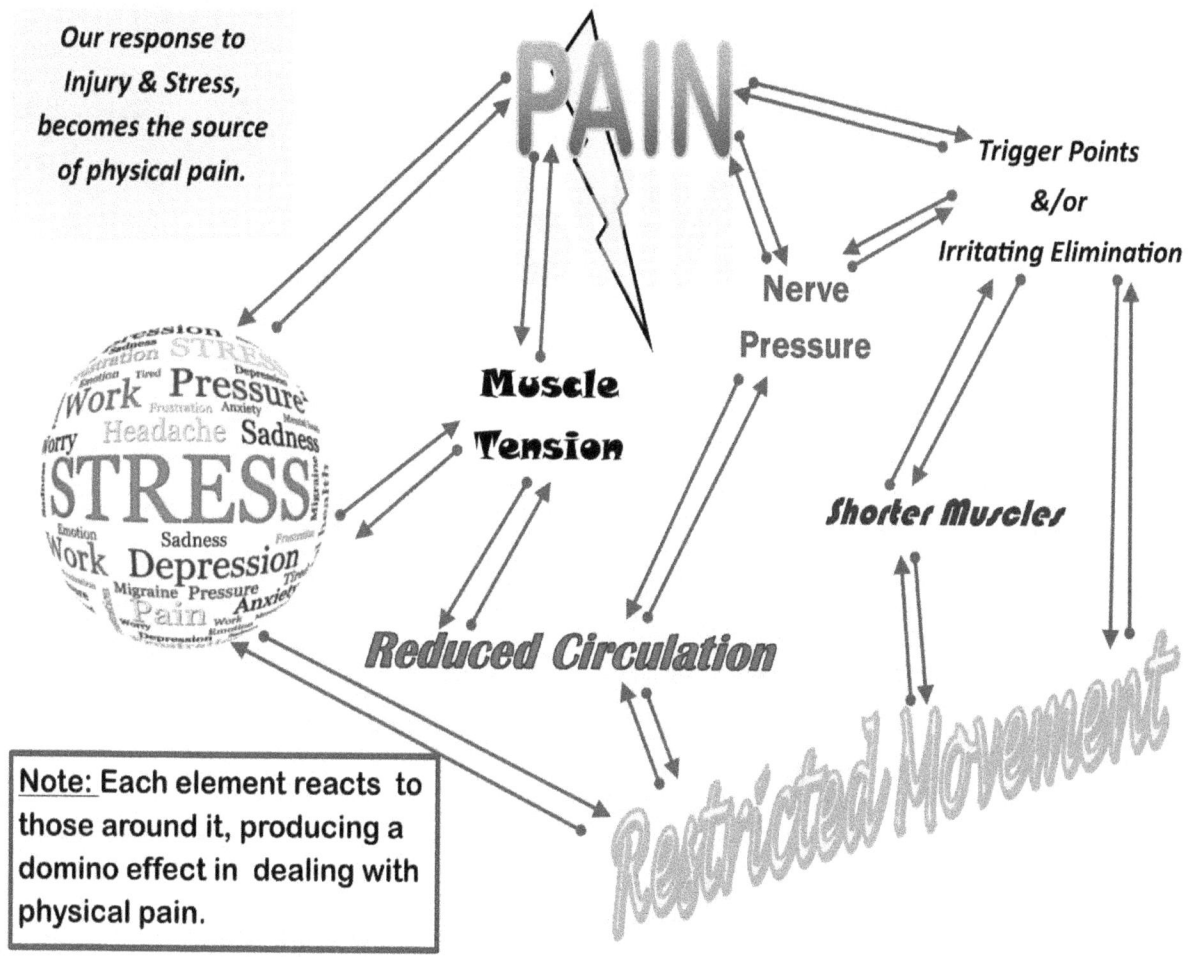

The word "somatic" refers to symptoms occurring within a person's body. In counseling, a somatic condition refers to a problem having its origin in an emotional problem. This concept is not a new one. John, the apostle, mentions it in III John, verse 2. "I would that you be in health even as your soul prospers."

An example of such would be seen in a client who suddenly experiences the onslaught of a debilitating migraine on a day when she is to reconcile with her estranged family. Such situations can be indicators of Fear, sometimes even when the client is unaware. If such a person were to compartmentalize their emotions, depending completely upon logic and reason, it is doubtful if actual processing toward healing would have occurred. The presence of the migraine confirms that indication, as well as the fragility of the client's emotional state.

Long-term somatic symptoms are indications of much deeper issues. The longer their presence in a client's life, the deeper the influence upon thoughts, choices and actions.

Section Three

Assessing Sources of Fear

Stress Point Scale

Life's pressures can have an effect on your physical health. The following scale, developed by a medical doctor, measures the relative impact of a variety of stressful events. Check the events that have occurred to you within the last twelve months and then add up the numerical value attached to each of the events. If an event took place more than once, (ie. Job change, etc.) be sure to add points for each instance.

Life Events	**Value**	**Your Score**
Death of a spouse	100	
Divorce	100	
Marital separation	75	
Jail term	65	
Death of a close family member	75	
Personal injury or illness	50	
Marriage	50	
Retirement	50	
Change in health of family member	45	
Pregnancy	45	
Sexual difficulties	44	
Gain of a new family member (in house)	40	
Gain of new family member (extended)	15	
Business adjustment (merger, downsizing, etc.)	39	

Change in financial status	38	_____
Death of a close friend	38	_____
Change to a different kind of work	36	_____
Change in communications with significant other	36	_____
Mortgage or loan more than $100,000	31	_____
Foreclosure of mortgage or loan	30	_____
Change in responsibilities at work	29	_____
Son or daughter leaving home	29	_____
Son or daughter moving back home	29	_____
Trouble with extended family	29	_____
Outstanding personal achievement	28	_____
Spouse changing job situation	26	_____
Beginning school	26	_____
End of school year	26	_____
Change in living conditions	25	_____
Revision of personal habits	24	_____
Difficulty with boss	23	_____
Change in work hours or conditions	20	_____
Change in residence	20	_____
Relocation/travel	20	_____
Change in schools	20	_____
Change in recreations	19	_____
Change in social activities	19	_____
Change in spiritual activities	19	_____

Loan for a major purchase (car, Appliance, school)	17	_____
Change in sleeping habits	16	_____
Change in number of family get-togethers	15	_____
Change in eating habits	15	_____
Vacation	13	_____
Christmas/Chanukah	12	_____
Minor violation of the law	11	_____
Court appearance	10	_____
TOTAL		_____
		_____

If your score is 250 or more, you are at a very high stress level, and probably run a major risk of illness in the next year. If your score is 150-200, your stress and illness risk are moderate. If you score between 75 and 150, your stress risks are mild.

The Problem of Stress vs. Performance

Stress has become an accepted element in our culture. In fact, many employers make Stress Management Assessment a required part of job placement. For our purposes, then, we find ourselves considering a person's personal levels of Fear when considering his/her Stress levels. Within the process of personal development, each of us must learn what levels are healthy and unhealthy in regard to our personal performance.

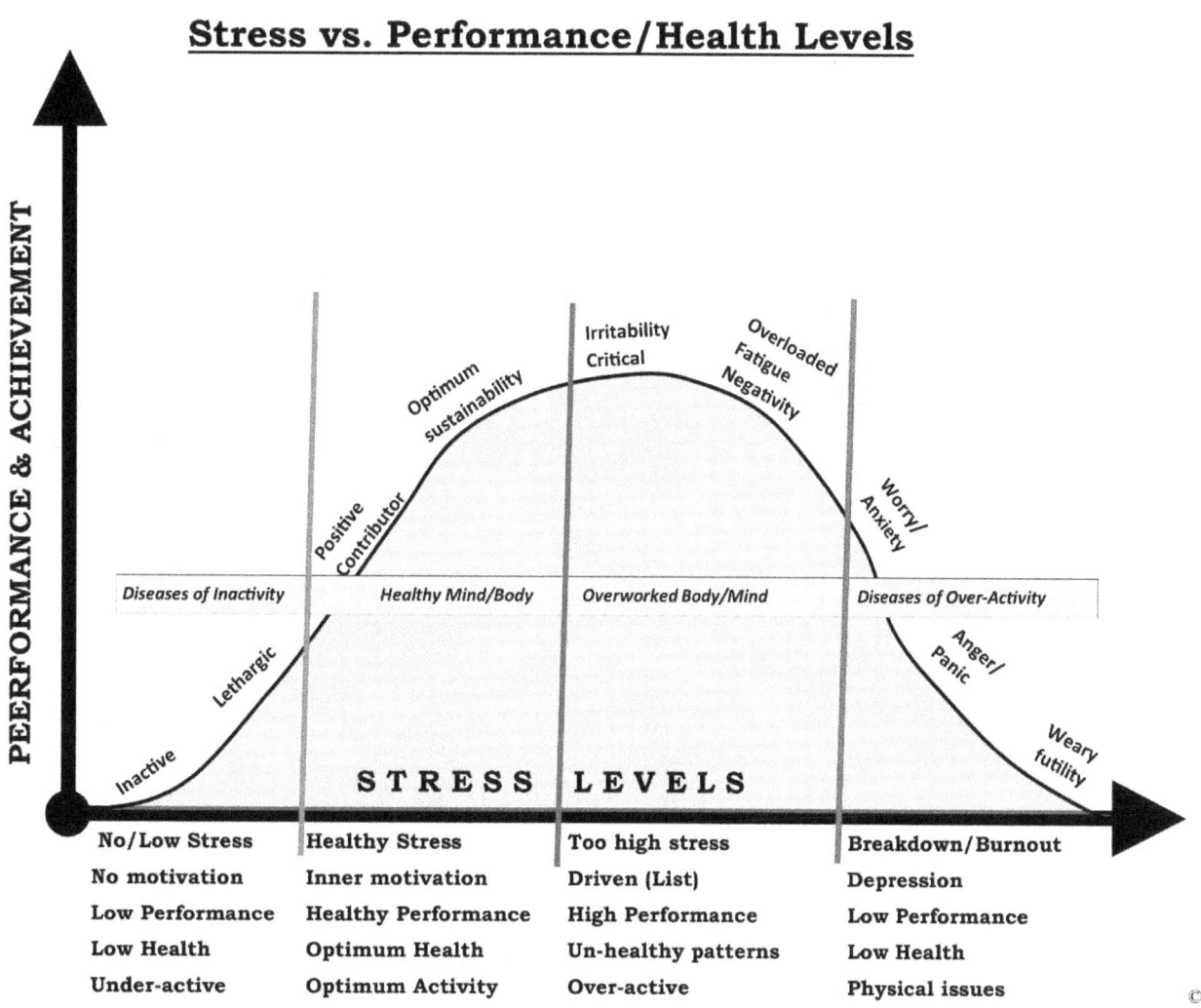

The human need for approval and acceptance can serve as a catalyst for what I call "Achievement Thinking." Achievement Thinking is based in competition and the carnal desire to hold "first place."

The effects of this type of thinking can be seen as a basis for family behaviors, sports' team structures, as well as in the business and professional arenas. Almost everyone on the planet has been exposed to this type of social structure. Many of us have had the experience of finding our place "outside" the relationship circle, and working that much harder to be approved and accepted.

Such relational and achievement responses serve as personal drivers. These can become a bondage which destroy a person's ability to experience a sense of personal rest. It certainly creates difficulty in the journey of the Christian disciple, who is encouraged in Scripture to cast cares and anxieties upon

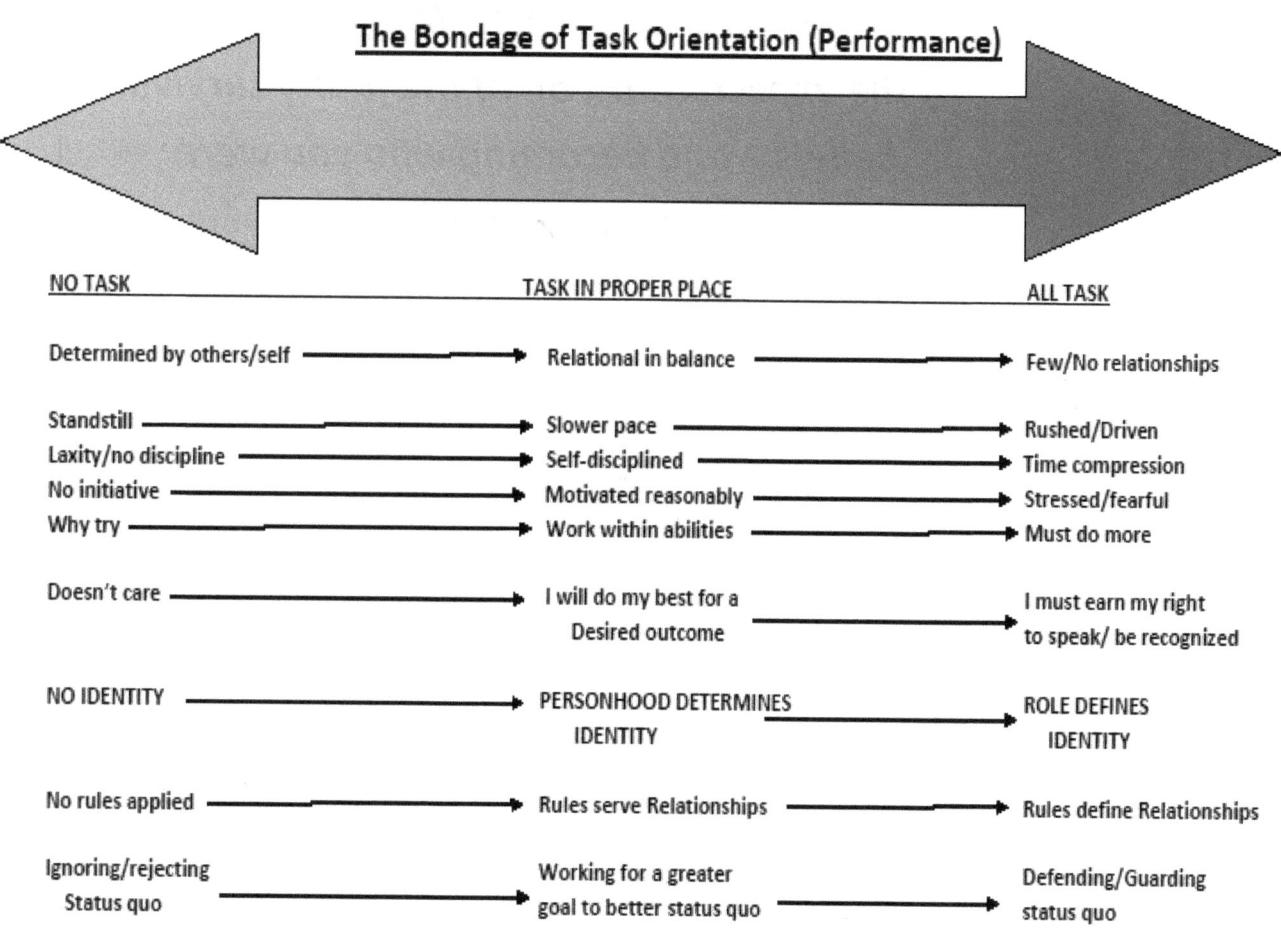

©2011 dcg/atg

> *"Healing may not be so much about getting better, as much it is about letting go of everything that isn't God's design for you – all of the expectations, all of the faulty survival beliefs – and becoming who you were created to become."*

Elements of a Survivor/Hidden Self Identity

From the moment of man's choice to sin in Eden, we have learned to hide our true selves. We have learned to measure our success and/or failure by our perceptions of the relationships around us. When Fear draws us into Performance Orientation, and we become need driven (rather than led by the Shepherd of our souls), we become survivors.

In every social culture and sub-culture, there is a silent expectation upon ourselves and others of "keeping up appearances." This promotes a sense of image-based living, which ultimately distorts our values and destroys our true identity.

The "Ruling" Survivor and Fearful Child

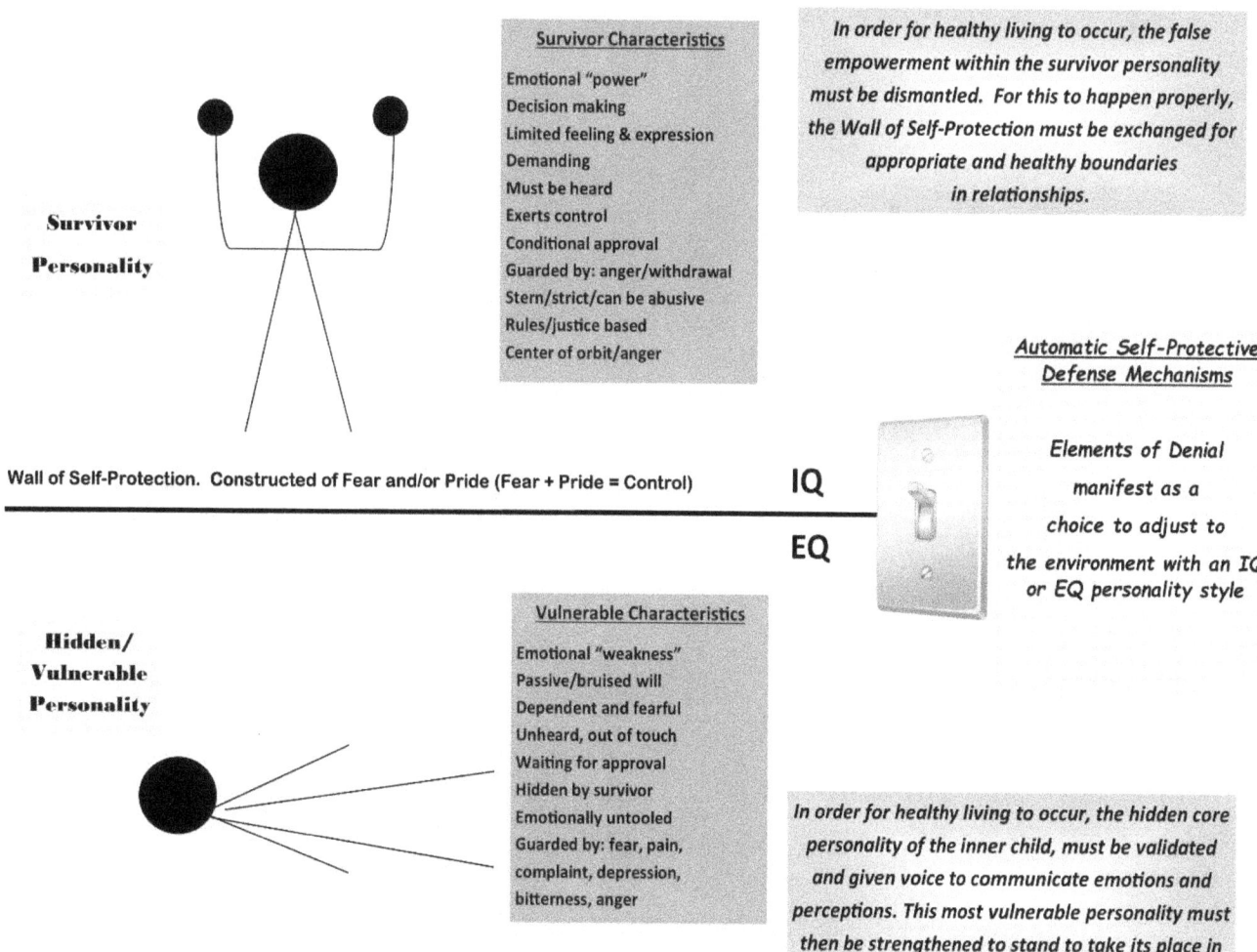

© dg/atg

Assessment: What is My Personal Level of Anxiety?

Next to each statement below, circle **Y** for *Yes*, **N** for *No*, or **S** for *Sometimes*.

Y	N	S	1. I expect others to treat me with respect
Y	N	S	2. I get anxious in shopping malls or stores.
Y	N	S	3. I get anxious eating or writing in front of others.
Y	N	S	4. I am uncomfortable speaking or performing in front of others.
Y	N	S	5. I worry about losing control of myself or my life.
Y	N	S	6. I am not excited about things the way I used to be.
Y	N	S	7. It's easy for me to develop an irritable mood.
Y	N	S	8. I worry I might embarrass myself or lose control in front of others.
Y	N	S	9. I tend to be a skeptical person.
Y	N	S	10. I rarely have enough energy.
Y	N	S	11. If I want something done right I feel I have to do it myself.
Y	N	S	12. It not unusual for me to feel angry for no apparent reason.
Y	N	S	13. I am uncomfortable going to the doctor or dentist, or hairdresser.
Y	N	S	14. I usually anticipate the worst-case scenario in most situations.
Y	N	S	15. I worry about doing certain things days before I actually do them.
Y	N	S	16. Things seem like just too much effort.
___	___	___	**Totals for this page**

Y	N	S	17. I've been known to take my anger out on others.
Y	N	S	18. I tend feel lonely on a regular basis.
Y	N	S	19. I feel better if I drink alcohol in a social situation.
Y	N	S	20. I experience stress if I am not in control of my life and my schedule.
Y	N	S	21. I have a hard time confronting others.
Y	N	S	22. I tend to take things very personally.
Y	N	S	23. I feel tired when I get up in the morning.
Y	N	S	24. I worry about what other people think of me.
Y	N	S	25. I tend to be critical of others and myself.
Y	N	S	26. I feel like I want to sleep all the time.
Y	N	S	27. I worry about irrational things happening to others or myself.
Y	N	S	28. I worry about getting sick or have stomach and bowel problems in public.
Y	N	S	29. I fear losing control in different areas of my life.
Y	N	S	30. I feel tired most of the time.
Y	N	S	31. I've been told that I react intensely in emotional situations.
Y	N	S	32. I don't feel comfortable in places where I can't come and go as I please.
Y	N	S	33. I worry about my health, i.e. disease, heart problems, illness.
___	___	___	**Totals for this page**

Y   N   S   34. I tend to see the negative side of a situation.

Y   N   S   35. I make excuses for not doing things or going places with others because of my anxiety.

Y   N   S   36. I have repetitive, worrisome, "what if" thoughts that I can't seem to turn off

Y   N   S   37. My mind races with scary or worrisome obsessive thoughts.

Y   N   S   38. I anticipate bad things happening to others or to myself me.

Y   N   S   39. I need to be in control of my surroundings to feel comfortable and/or safe.

Y   N   S   40. I have a difficulty sleeping, i.e. falling asleep, and staying asleep.

Y   N   S   41. I have a tendency to speak negatively about myself.

Y   N   S   42. I am concerned about my anger and irritability levels. I wish I was a nicer person.

Y   N   S   43. I worry about losing my mind or becoming mentally ill.

Y   N   S   44. I anticipate bad things happening to others or myself.

Y   N   S   45. I am uncomfortable driving or riding in cars.

Y   N   S   46. I worry about other people's opinions of me.

Y   N   S   47. I worry about my health

____   **Totals for this page**

Y	N	S	48. I tend to over-react to things emotionally
Y	N	S	49. I get mad at myself easily.
Y	N	S	50. I have a fear of germs and contamination.
Y	N	S	51. In certain situations I feel compelled to run out and get away.
Y	N	S	52. I feel sad many times for no apparent reason.
Y	N	S	53. I don't want to eat or I eat too much
Y	N	S	54. I tend to become irritated easily, especially when I'm stressed.
Y	N	S	55. I dread medical tests, physical exams, or visiting hospitals.
Y	N	S	56. I prefer to avoid public transportation such as buses, trains, planes, and such.
Y	N	S	57. I am emotional and cry easily most days.
Y	N	S	58. I feel uncomfortable and sometimes avoid closed in places such as elevators, airplanes, or large crowds.
Y	N	S	59. I don't feel in control of my emotions
Y	N	S	60. I am disappointed in others.
Y	N	S	61. I worry about myself.
Y	N	S	62. It's difficult for me to relax around people unless I am with my "safe" person.
Y	N	S	63. I struggle with feeling restless and wound up much of the time.
Y	N	S	64. I don't like to be alone

_____ **Totals for this page**

Y	N	S	65. I feel disappointed with my ability to live my life.
Y	N	S	66. Things don't turn out the way I think they should.
Y	N	S	67. I feel guilty easily.
Y	N	S	68. I apologize for things that aren't my fault.
Y	N	S	69. I find myself repeating behaviors such as washing my hands, checking locked doors, etc.
Y	N	S	70. I worry that I won't be prepared in an emergency.

___ ___ ___ **Totals for this page**

___ ___ ___ **Totals for questions 1-16**

___ ___ ___ **Totals for questions 17-33**

___ ___ ___ **Totals for questions 34-47**

___ ___ ___ **Totals for questions 48-64**

___ + ___ + ___ = _____ **Totals for all pages**

Please see the next page to review the key for your totals.

Key:

0-50 points   You deal with a minimal amount of anxiety, and are relatively healthy.

51-90 points   You struggle with more stress and anxiety that you really need to, and should seek help to make a few life-style changes. Its possible you have learned to absorb the stress and expectations around you. The patterns you have used to adapt to relationships need to be adjusted if you are to finish well.

91-140 points   Your stress and anxiety levels are in the danger zone. Not only should you seek some help in making some life-style changes, but you should have your health assessed by your medical physician and consider medication temporarily until you have been able to fully address the situations and relationships causing you difficulty. Its probably you are totally unaware of just how much you have been carrying in your life until now.

Defense Mechanisms Keeping Fear in Place

Guilt over our failures, and missed moments for relationship prevent freedom in our lives. Many times, we have been raised in environments where Guilt was used by others to prevent bad behaviors, or maintain relationships. In homes where dysfunction is the rule ("don't show, don't tell"), Guilt is known as "feeling bad." In Christian homes where dysfunction is the rule, we learn to transfer that faulty belief to our relationship with God. We somehow come to believe that God uses Guilt to keep us in line.

When we are healthy, we recognize that God doesn't use Guilt to motivate us. In fact, His desire is to draw us to Himself for acceptance, forgiveness, healing and growth. There is nothing of rejection or conditional responses in His reaching-out toward us.

He is God, and He does not change.

His is not the attitude of a Judgmental Overseer, nor that of favoritism and partiality. He came to give us LIFE – Healthy Life – HIS Life. Giving and Relationship have always been HIS PLAN.

Community was His idea.

He is LOVE.

Six Types of Guilt

1. **Good and reasonable guilt –** what we feel when we violate God's law; when we sin against God and others; when we deal with consequences. (Our conscience speaks, based upon Spirit of God, making us hungry for Him and for relationship and instruction.)

2. **Deserved guilt** – what we feel when we fail in daily life, "I forgot to feed the dog," "I neglected to clean the bathroom," etc. (Fear of disapproval based upon rules of your family of origin.)

3. **"Hamster Wheel" Guilt** -- when we violate self-imposed rules, deadlines, etc. "I didn't get it all done today." (Fear of disapproval based upon lack of achievement; performance)

4. **Borrowed Guilt** – when we violate what we have been taught we "should" do. (Fear of failing due to the inability to maintain a certain "image" – this type of guilt is directly linked to the manipulations of shame.)

5. **Imposed Guilt** – when we allow others to violate our personal values and boundaries: others communicate their expectations upon us in a condemning manner. We succumb to the pressure and modify who we are based upon their opinion. (fear of disapproval and loss of relationship.)

6. **Guilty Hindsight** – when we take responsibility for what we might have done differently, or prevented. We judge our past selves based upon our present knowing. (Fear of God's judgment and rejection from others because we think we are expected to "know" what we were never taught.)

The only one of these forms of guilt that is positive in our lives is the first one – and Jesus came to cover that.

Unhealthy Guilt is the source of most of our emotional & spiritual distractions.

Shame:
Fear's not-so-distant Cousin

Shame is a sense of foreboding that can follow a person an entire lifetime. It is a dark sense of failure which cannot seem to be pin-pointed with a cause. Shame works like a filter on a person's understanding, keeping them from assessing their Creator-provided value. Continually, they apologize, even when the circumstances they apologize for are not a result of their choices, words, or actions.

In fact, Shame's filter dictates to a person that they are on the "outside," and could never be truly loved or accepted because something is wrong with them; something that cannot be repaired or made to work properly.

When Shame couples with Fear, a person experiences deep emotions of failure and trepidation. They will struggle with believing or trusting others, and will continually expect efforts and expectations to fail. They will compensate for their own sense of inadequacy by seeking please others (as the hidden true self). Or, they will compensate by seeking to rule others and control their environment (as the survivor).

©dg/atg

How Do We Learn to Nurture Shame?

Models of Authority (↓ parents)	Actions	Message the child receives
1. Untrained authority figures; Not ready for the job	1. Does not know what childhood should look like. 2. Image based; worried about what people think. 3. Expect child to be a small adult 4. Unreasonable expectations; perfectionism 5. Expects the child to already know 6. "You should know better" 7. "What's wrong with you?" 8. "Where did you learn to act like that?"	1. I can't measure up 2. I have to figure things out alone 3. I'll never be good enough 4. There's something wrong with me that I can't fix.
2. Pre-occupied authority figures; Not seeing the importance of the job	1. Emotionally distant; no heart connection 2. Pre-occupied with work, activities, addiction 3. Child is drawn into the orbit around parents 4. Too busy for play; disinterested 5. Doesn't attend child's events 6. No celebration of effort 7. Work oriented achievement/Performance 8. Always time crunched; no quantity time	1. My needs don't matter 2. Others are more important than me 3. I'm not important enough 4. There's no one for me 5. I'm in the way 6. I have less worth than others
3. Exploitative authority figures; Not willing to account for the outcome of the job.	1. Abuse – knowingly, or unknowingly 2. Hands off – verbal, emotional, financial – intimidation, withdrawal, control 3. Hands on – physical, sexual	1. I shouldn't be here 2. I don't belong – I'm outside 3. I'm not wanted 4. I'm not worth it – I have no value 5. There's something wrong with me I can't fix.

0-5 years

Magical Thinking = "I caused the events in my world; happily ever after; everyone needs to be happy"

Self-Concept = The way I fit into the world (learned in pre-cognitive years); from cues and signals received by those in relationship. What works for my survival

Models and Imprintings for adult life

"I will become the one who has hurt me the most, because I am bound by my pain. My focus becomes my blockage to growth."

Messages of "Toxic Shame" or "False Guilt"

"There is something wrong with me that makes me worth-less than others."

Qualities of Control

Seeks to set criteria for acceptance and relationship
Feels it is owed due to what it feels it has given

Overt Control
(Visible)
Examples:

Russian KGB
Chinese Communist Government
Military Surveillance

1. Imprisonment (emotional or physical)
2. Humiliation
3. Embarrassment (shame)
4. Coercion
5. Mandated communication
6. Bullying/Anger/ Threats to cause
7. Invalidation, conditional validation
8. Spirit of disregard of a person's identity
9. Demanding information/must know
10. Seeking the limitation of others through physical, verbal or emotional restraint

Subverted Control
(Under the surface)
Examples:

Spoiled Child
Crippled Grandmother
Image Consultant

1. Self Pity/ Pouting
2. Responding with Victimization/ Accusation
3. Guilt
4. Continual rehearsal of problem
5. With-holding of response—wants for other person to come to them.
6. Requiring persuasion or placation
7. Speaking for, or acting for another person without asking to know their heart
8. Blame/Communicated fear of loss of image
9. Creating indispensability
10. Manipulation of circumstance or others' knowledge of circumstance

PRIDE

"But he gives more grace. Wherefore he said, "God resists the proud, but gives grace to the humble. Submit yourselves therefore to God. Resist the devil, and he will flee from you. Draw nigh to God, and he will draw night to you. ... Humble yourselves in the sight of the Lord, and he shall lift you up." James 4:6-10

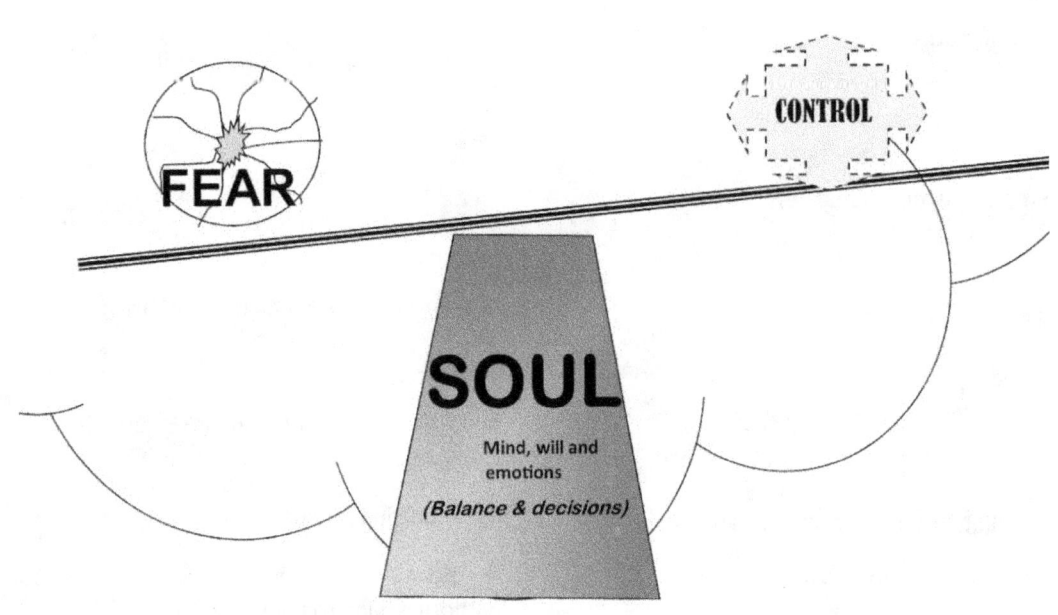

Spiritual Implications of Fear Issues

When we are afraid, we cover ourselves.
Loss of experiential relationship with our Creator is the real
Root of our Fear Problems.
See Genesis 3:8-11

Fear causes us to run – it drives us –

The Father leads us by His Spirit.

Fear causes us to trust circumstances –
Crises and adrenaline push us to action

Love leads us to trust relationship
and to wait for direction

Definitions of Counseling Terms, in light of Spiritual Truth:

Depression: Fear has caused us to buy into a false belief that we are alone, and without hope.

Denial Blindness and/or resistance to humbly admit our need.

Insecurity Our subconscious awareness that we are handling the unknown in our own strength without the Father's strength as our source.

Perfectionism Trying to be perfect in our own efforts.

Self-Hatred Expecting ourselves to be perfect without a provided growth pattern. We have made ourselves our own source, and have realized that we are unable to meet our own needs; we blame ourselves for our insufficiency and for our mistakes. "If I can just be like *that*."

Avoidance Trying to solving it ourselves; finding temporary fixes, and then bouncing on to the next thing we try. Closing relationships when we feel forced to face our own pain, bringing change.

Giving and Receiving Love – Filters and Motivations

Receives the Love of God & applies it to own heart	Motivated & Influenced by Fear	Motivated & Influenced by Pride
1. Operates in discernment	1. Operates in suspicion	1. Operates in assumptions
2. Is a disciple – ask questions	2. Follows without questions	2. Makes statements; has to already "understands"
3. Trusts with an open heart	3. Is afraid to trust; creates situations to avoid change	3. Moves independently; sees no need to trust others
4. Seeks community; sees a need for personal growth	4. Anticipates repetition of prior wounds	4. Admits no vulnerability
5. Is teachable – with arguments or debate	5. Desires to be taught, but thinks growth is unattainable	5. Always has answers; must "know," and be seen as having it all together
6. Seeks to change self	6. Wants others to change them-- afraid to take steps on their own is afraid to fail	6. Seeks to change others, while applying no change personally
7. Is willing to wait patiently	7. Gives up when no results are seen quickly – assumes failure	7. Manipulates circumstances for desired outcome
8. Has no agenda	8. Must have control of their own environment	8. Must have personal rights acknowledged
9. Responds kindly	9. Guarded responses/silence	9. Unfeeling responses; factual
10. Accepts responsibility for own mistakes	10. Blames self	10. Blames others
11. Receives love unconditionally	11. Must reciprocate to keep a balance – fears rejection. Argues with love/forgiveness of God.	11. Sets criteria in order to be loved – sets terms and conditions Actions not on the personal "list" are not seen as love. Argues with love of God. Must earn significance.
12. Gives love unconditionally	12. Loves in order to find acceptance. Expressed gratitude/ apologies are deemed as undeserved	12. Loves in order to gain control expressed gratitude/apologies are deemed as not good enough.
13. Operates relationally	13. Anticipates Rejection	13. Operates alone. Has no real need for others.
14. Keeps no record of wrongs	14. Keeps a list of personal wounds, to confirm and reinforce stalled growth	14. Keeps a list of others' failings to maintain sense of superior standing – holds others "accountable." Makes demands.
I Corinthians 13/ Psalm 103 Sees God as a Loving Father Accepts Grace; gives Grace	*John 5:1-9/II Timothy 1:7 – Sees God as chess player. Is crippled in heart and feels inwardly broken. Is waiting for "Perfect Timing."*	*James 4:1-10/I Peter 2:11-25 – Sees God as the Ultimate Control, overpowering His people. Person is Blind and deaf, trying to "find his own way." Battles with anger and frustration.*

©dcg,at

Attitudes Reflecting Fear's Trademark

Make a mark next to the statements you agree with.

_____I must be perfect in my attitudes and appearance or I will be rejected.

_____If I make a mistake, something horrible will happen.

_____If I do things perfectly, I will be accepted.

_____If I don't do things "right" I will be embarrassed.

_____When I get it right, I will finally accept myself.

_____If others do not approve of me, then I am not okay.

_____If authority figures accept and approve of me, then I am spiritually okay.

_____I don't think I will ever be good enough.

_____Things should be done the right way.

_____If I do things well, I will be noticed and accepted.

_____When things go wrong, I need to fix them so everyone will be happy.

_____It falls to me to keep the peace in my home.

_____I must keep a clean environment. Order brings approval.

_____When I make mistakes, I feel worthless.

_____I cannot allow myself to fail.

_____God accepts me when I have covered all of my bases.

If you identified with more than 5 of these statements, it signifies you have allowed Fear defense mechanisms to affect how you allow yourself to receive love from God and others.

The possible causes of anxiety and fear are many: Conflict, health problems, dangerous situations, death, unmet needs, spiritual problems, false beliefs, etc.

"According to the Bible, there is nothing wrong with realistically acknowledging and trying to deal with the identifiable problems of life. To ignore danger is fooling and wrong. But it is also wrong, as well as unhealthy, to be immobilized by excessive worry. Such worry must be committed to prayer to God, who can release us from paralyzing fear or anxiety, and free us to deal realistically with the needs and welfare both of others and of ourselves." (Dr. Gary R. Collins, *Christian Counseling*, p. 66.)

Judge or Assessor (and Healer?)
Fear Takes Hold Because We Anticipate Judgment

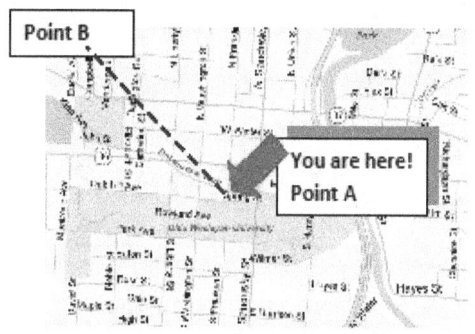

Assessment

Main Focus: Living in Right Relationship

Point B – Health
Point A – Present Location

Before a pathway can be charted to a final destination of health and development, we must assess or appraise where we are presently living. Without a proper appraisal, it is impossible to map out a straight line; creating personal application of the need for growth.

Results:
Truth/reality speaks
Emotional awareness
Healing of memories
Grief is processed
Facilitates growth and healing

Judgment

Good or Bad
Pass or Fail
Right or Wrong
Win or Lose

Main Focus: Lawful Living

Judgment attaches a *negative moral value* to the "You are Here" mechanism and closes the gate to growth/change.

Results:
Negative emotions speak/control
Numbness of heart
Repressed memories
Stalled grief cycle
Stops growth and healing

© atg/dcg

Attributes of Judgment and/or Assessment

*How do you believe God (Jesus)
and His Body (the church)
will respond in relationship to you?*

Assessment
"GOD IS MY HEALER AND FRIEND"

Abba Father views us through the eyes of assessment, seeing our places of pain as potential meeting places for comfort and healing.

Elements of Assessment

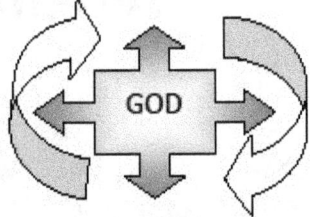

1. Assigns value to people because they carry the image of God within themselves – either with Jesus or without Him.

2. Operates through a heart-choice of love, trust, community, and mutual safety.

3. Uses potential and relationship to motivate; Holy Spirit led, serving based; Kingdom order.

4. What a person does flows from who they are becoming.

5. Weakness and mistakes are expected elements of learning

6. Abba Father based, Spirit derived, relationship centered

7. Acceptance and approval are centered in the unconditional and unfailing love of God—all people are equal.

Judgment
"GOD IS A HARD MAN, WAITING FOR ME TO MESS UP"

We view ourselves through the eyes of judgment, seeing our places of pain as places of potential rejection, disapproval and ultimate rejection by God. Positions of power are maintained through authority, posturing, and intimidation.

Elements of Judgment

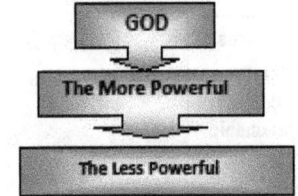

1. Assigns value to people based upon beauty, achievement, success, health, brains, and ability

2. Operates through a mindset of authority, hierarchy, Political power, religious traditions & institutional organization.

3. Uses fear to motivate; performance driven; man's order

4. What a person does is more important than who they are

5. Weakness and mistakes diminish value /unacceptable

6. Man based; Intellect derived, rules/tradition centered

7. Rejection and disapproval of those who are different than the common group

© atg/dcg

How Fear Takes Hold

*"For God has not given us
a spirit of fear, but of power,
and of love, and of a sound mind."
II Timothy 1:7*

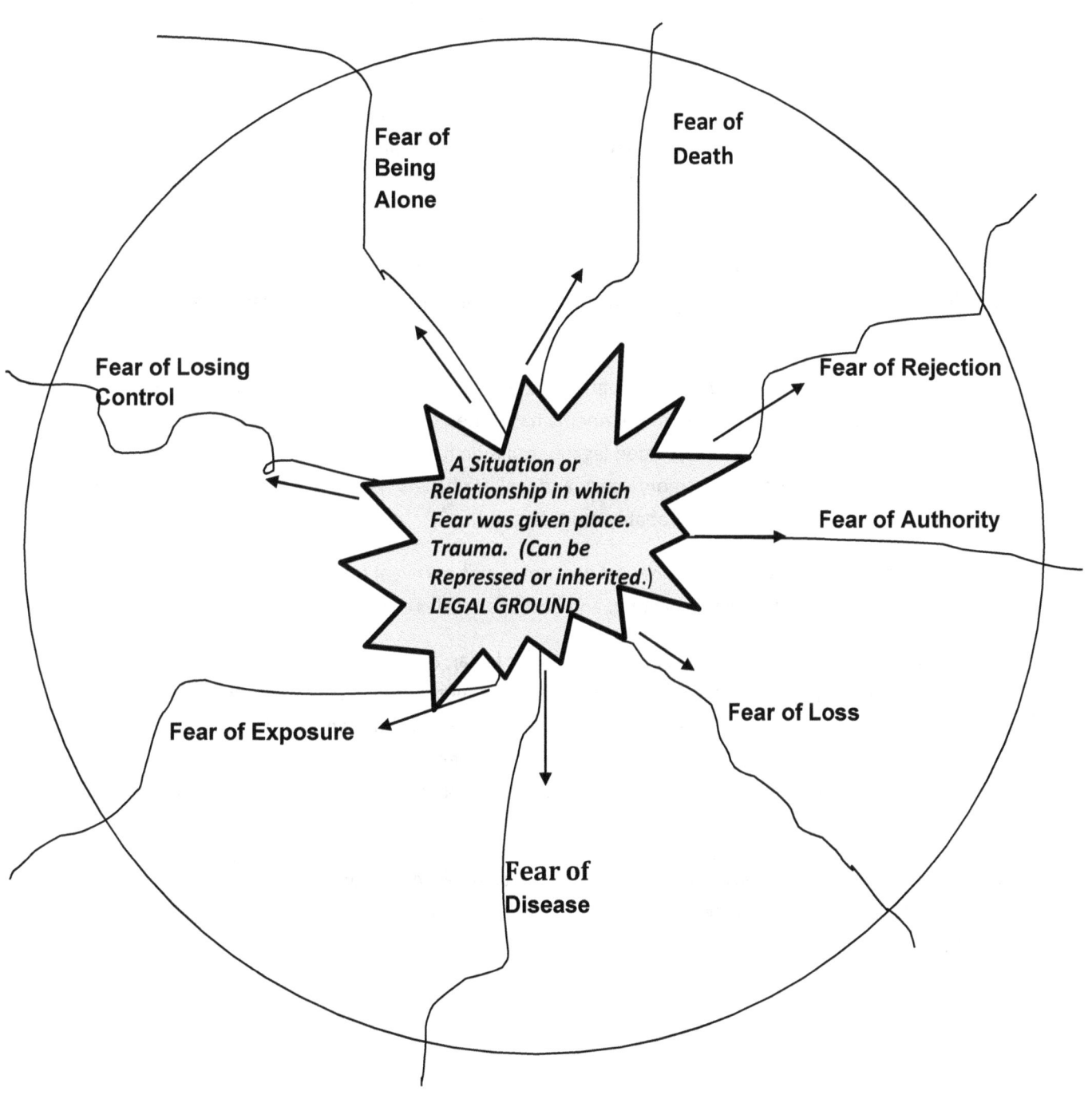

How To Expose and Break the Power of Fear

*"For God has not given us
a spirit of fear, but of power,
and of love, and of a sound mind."*
II Timothy 1:7

1. A situation occurs, usually traumatic, which opens a door for fear and torment within the soul. The circumstance is either re-lived, or is repressed, depending upon the person's ability to deal with it at the given time. In a person's emotions, a spiritual "tap root" begins to grow from the seed of the trauma. The root begins to "flavor" the soil in the soul, beginning the stronghold of Fear in a person's life.

2. The wound remains open within the soul, continuing to influence choices made in various life-areas. Eventually, it sends out "runners" within the soul that are evidenced as varying forms of fear.

3. Rather than deal with each individual attribute of fear, it is better to go after the traumatic memory, which is the legal ground the enemy has gained to torment the person. (In the blindness of pain, the person provided legal permission for Fear's torment to begin to be accommodated.) Take that memory apart, and look for beliefs the person's "bought into" during that moment. (The beliefs are probably multi-faceted).

4. Move slowly, not with zeal alone. Ask the Holy Spirit to reveal the traumatic circumstance. This will take some time, some waiting, and perhaps a little researching of life history.

5. Pray. Repent for opening the door to the spirit of Fear, and for giving it place, by accommodating it. Renounce its legal hold. Cut off generational ties to fear within the family, which have served to make it stronger, and have reinforced its influence and ability to rule the life. Forgive those who were involved in exposing the person to Fear. Release the right to hold on the attributes of fear as part of the personality. Apply the Blood of Jesus Christ. Anoint with oil, and break the yoke of bondage.

6. Apply intentional choices and actions to make changes in life-style from this point forward. The person will feel weak initially, and need coaching, counseling, and community to maintain their freedom in Christ.

The Difference between Conviction and Condemnation

Conviction	*Condemnation*
(The work of the Holy Spirit, creating healthy Development and growth – invokes a desire to Follow and learn)	*(The work of Hell's minions, creating an umbrella of rejection, disapproval and religious judgment.)*
(creates right relationship)	sees problems (drives away)

Conviction	Condemnation
1. Causes a person to flee into the Presence of God. "Running to see Dad and talk things out."	1. Hinders approach to God. Afraid of His responses.
2. Aids in walking with God. Knowledge of being justified.	2. Hinders fellowship with God. "He doesn't want to spend time with me, I'm not good enough."
3. Failure and sin are removed, to greatly help fellowship with the Father.	3. Looks at failures as grounds for having no rights to God's fellowship. However, it never removes those failures.
4. Although conviction can cause you to feel miserable until you pray and repent, it is very specific in its dealing.—a specific instance requires a specific response. Conviction contains NO REJECTION.	4. Condemnation comes as an over-all general put-down. A person doesn't feel a sense of approval; just "bad," and not enough all over. Condemnation invokes a tendency to compare yourself with others and always come up short.
Psalm 139:23-24. It is the Holy Spirit's job to search your heart. You cannot search and deal with all of your life's issues alone, and then present what you have found to Father God.	**Romans 8:1-2.** Christ does not operate in condemnation, but in the law of the Spirit of Life. **Ephesians 1** – He wants us to walk in understanding of His Plan and destiny for each of our lives.
Jeremiah 17:10 **II Corinthians 5:17**	
CLEANSING!!	**BURDENING!!**
End result = *PEACE*	End result = *GUILT/SHAME*
I John 1:9	**Psalm 32:3**

Whatever you are not willing to confront

you are willing to live with.

Section Four.

The Counselor's Role in Helping Those Who Struggle with Fear

When a client presents in a counselor's office with issues of any kind, it is of primary importance to counselor establish a trustworthy relationship with that client. Clients who face difficulties with Fear, are in specific need of comfort and reassurance. It is important to allow the client to share their story, and explain why they think are afraid. In hearing their description of events, you will gain insight and clues to help the person come to discovery as to the root of their Fear issues.

To break the ice with fear, it is sometimes a good idea to go through the following questions with the client verbally, asking for a rating of

1	for	*never true*
2	for	*rarely true*
3	for	*sometimes true*
4	for	*rarely true*
5	for	*always true*

Evaluation Statements

1. I get stressed pretty easily. Score_____
2. I feel as though I am always worried about something. Score_____
3. I feel depressed often Score_____
4. The things I worry about many times are thing others consider unimportant Score_____
5. It doesn't take much for me to panic. Score_____
6. I tend to experience unexpected thoughts that can take over my mind. Score_____
7. Things bother me pretty easily. Score_____
8. I tend to worry about things even when they are no longer a threat. Score_____
9. I am insecure in new situations Score_____
10. I have physical symptoms in addition to the Anxiety I deal with. Score_____

Evaluation Key:

17 or below   Transitory anxiety

19-27   Moderate anxiety

28-36   Significant anxiety

37 and above High anxiety

Depending upon the outcome of this little verbal assessment, you will have a clue as to how to proceed in helping your client come to health.

Persons who deal with Fear, experience what is called "inner dialogue." Expressions of perceived conflict show in an escalation of emotional intensity. This chart explains those levels, and can help your client to be able to understand their own level of health in dealing with Fear.

Levels of Intensity in Conflict

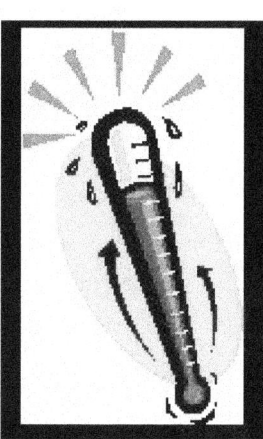

0 -- No conflict; no fear; no sense of discomfort

1 -- Small disturbance in personal peace levels; no permanent issues

2 -- A sense of agitation; irritation with an event or person; kept within self.

3 -- Stifled anger; subconscious need to protect self

4 -- A greater sense of agitation; voiced irritation with an event or person; sharing anger or frustration.

5 -- Complaint; Visible self-protection; Inner urge to withdraw.

6 -- Recurring concern; Focus of difficulty intrudes on daily thoughts.

7 -- Sensing a need to make a change – driven; sense of urgency (more often)

8 -- Constantly nagging worry; feeling driven to fix something; hyper-responsibility

9 -- Very stressed; no sleep; feeling unequipped to address the concern; overwhelmed

10 -- Feels the end of life as we know it; everything is about to fall apart

Concepts to Help You Reach Your Client
Look through the following general suggestions for the counseling office. Each one represents a lesson learned over the past 30 years or so. It is my hope to provide you with an approach or line of thinking you can follow in order to help your client relax and begin to trust in learning about healthy living.

1. Listen to your client's story. When do they remember their symptoms happening for the first time? Are they experiencing Fear symptoms without memories to explain them? If they do have memories, do they experience Fear symptoms each time they think of the event?

2. Prior to coming to your office, were the memories tied to the Fear symptoms repressed? Move forward slowly and be very careful in your questioning. Be gentle. People who deal with issues of Fear need comfort and assurance, and emotionally fragile. There is a reason why the memories evoke pain, and/or why they were repressed.

3. As the discoveries occur and more history comes to light, be sure to cover the steps you have made together with prayer. Pray with your client. Bind up every form of torment. Take communion with them. Give assignments to help their will to heal, and reinforce what God is doing.

4. Remind your client of the progress they have made, by recounting steps verbally. Emotional development happens slowly, and is much like physical therapy. The client needs to do the work, but it is painful, and they must be reminded and supported in order to discover their own resolve to grow. Encourage and wait – impatience and frustration only suggest to the client that their original reasons for distrust and self-protection were correct in the first place. Ask them to journal discoveries and emotions

5. Simplify and break down the steps you perceive need to be taken. Communicate bite-sized pieces for growth to the client, to help them to recognize their forward movement. Goals must be Measurable, Achievable, Personal and Specific. (Remember MAPS) This prevents discouragement from setting in.

6. When you perceive a problem in your client's thinking, or choices, turn your perception into a question. Questions using "Why" or "How" invoke more open responses, and help deepen the communication happening in the office. Even if you are sure of a solution, take the client there with guided questions.

7. At times, you will need to give short lessons of instruction, in order to explain a concept. It is best to use illustrations and keep the lessons short, as most clients need to verbally process what they are learning. NEVER PREACH – as this creates a sense of being condescended to in an individual's mind. Always approach your clients with respect for their experiences.

8. Try to restate the solutions presenting themselves from a variety of perspectives. This will invoke creative learning on the part of the client, and help them to make better connections with the lessons they are learning. It is a good idea to use re-statements to make sure what you have said has been understood.

9. Keep notes on your client's sessions, even if they are bulleted statements added to a file. Every person feels closer to a person who remembers the story that is important to them.

Stress/Anxiety Management Techniques

Utilize these concepts one at a time, teaching them to clients who deal with Fear Symptoms. As one technique is learned, add another, until an arsenal is developed in the client, enabling confidence. Practice the concept with them in session, and remind them when they are experiencing symptoms, similar to the method used in coaching a woman through labor.

1. When anxiety begins to occur, help your client to recognize the physical symptoms as warning signs. For example, blood pressure begins to rise, muscles in the neck and shoulders tighten, pulse increases, cheeks might become warm/flushed, and a sense of insecurity or confusion might begin to manifest inwardly. Help them become aware of these indicators. Teach them to take a deep breath, hold it, and then exhale very slowly. This technique will slow body processes, and help them to calm.

2. Teach your client to think about their favorite place and silently pray, when Fear symptoms begin. Teach them to make a conscious choice not to become upset, or believe the thoughts presenting themselves within. Help them not to allow dignity and energy to be spent when it isn't necessary.

3. When overcome with anxiety, help your client to slow down in their speech patterns. This helps regain a sense of personal management and normalcy.

4. Help your client by breaking down responsibilities they might feel are looming overhead. Assign 2 items to be completed between sessions. It is essential they follow through with at least one thing. Remember MAPS. Many times, a client is overwhelmed for good reason.

5. If weather permits, encourage a walk during session. Help your client choose to talk a walk outside, or at least sit outside their own home and read, for a minimum of five minutes. Encourage them to do this 2-3 times between sessions. And end goal might be to embolden them to participate in more structured exercise; first at home, then at a gym.

6. Help your client work towards healthy nutrition. Begin by helping the client to drink water, and eat small nutritious snack. Anxiety can be brought on by dehydration and poor nourishment.

7. Teach your client to reward successes with a treat for soul care; perhaps an ice cream cone, or renting a movie they've wanted to see, a bubble bath, going fishing, reading a book for an hour. There are just a few suggestions. Add a few low cost choices of your own. The only rule regarding these rewards; they must be used without being mixed with errands, chores, or other responsibilities.

8. Help your client to get to the root of any anger issues which are, many times, based in personal justice issues. Help them process the pain under those issues, and work with them in letting go of those who caused the hurt and injustice in their lives.

9. Help your client to rub away stress. There are three key areas of the human body a person can massage to alleviate much of one's own stress.

    a. Hands – rub together, palm to palm, and apply hand lotion. A pressure point located between the thumb and first finger is directly related to nerve points in the back of the neck. Sometimes, repeated hard pressure for several seconds at a time, can alleviate stress, or related pain.
    b. Head – using fingertips to rub the temples, work in circular motion. Place an ice pack at the back of the neck, just under the skull cap and lean back. Press two pressure points at the top of the nose, pressing with the thumbs towards the back of the head into the sinuses.
    c. Feet – Massage lotion into the feet. Soak in water.

10. Help your client to take a break from virtual networks, computers, movies and televisions. There is stress relief in old school life-styles. Draw a picture. Paint. Do a crossword puzzle. Detach from the constant chatter of media. This helps to re-engage with our identity as human, rather than machine.

11. Encourage your client to make a list of positive things that have happened in his/her life. These can serve as a sort of "string of pearls" to read over when things go back.

12. Help your client to re-program thought patterns when they are in the middle of a difficult situation. In every crisis, there is at least one positive thing to be observed in the midst of it. I call this the "Silver Lining Principle." Even in the darkest of times, there will be one thing to give thanks for. Persons who struggle with negativity need help to re-program their thinking patterns. The discipline of looking for the positive requires hard work. This step can actually work better on a client's behalf than medications.

"Now may our Lord Jesus Christ Himself,
and our God and Father, who has loved us
and given us everlasting consolation
and good hope by grace, comfort your hearts
and establish you in every good word and work."
(2 Thessalonians 2:16-17)

Section Five.

Required Choices to Heal

How to Determine What Is Speaking to You

What God says

When God speaks, the message is accompanied by a sense of approval and affirmation.

We tend to relate to God based on our learning style.

We know we are loved, and personally known.

We feel protected.

He speaks the truth.

He teaches us.

He encourages us.

He gives us understanding.

He gives us direction.

What Self says

When Self speaks, the message is usually focused on our own places of pain. We typically think in "I" statements.

Self says things like:

"I feel _____."

"I wish _____."

Discovery Keys

1. Stop whatever you are doing. Stand/sit still to think.

2. Focus on what's happening inside you. (think these 3 columns.)

3. Pray in the Spirit. Ask God to help you.

4. Ask Jesus to rescue you and show you what you are hearing.

5. Let your heart relax and receive the love of God for you in that situation.

What Fear says

When Fear speaks, the message is accompanied by a sense of failure, futility and intimidation. Fear typically speaks in "you" statements.

Fear says things like:

"What if _____."

"You'll never _____."

"What's wrong with you?"

"You should _____."

"You can't _____."

©2011 dcg/atg

Determination Chart

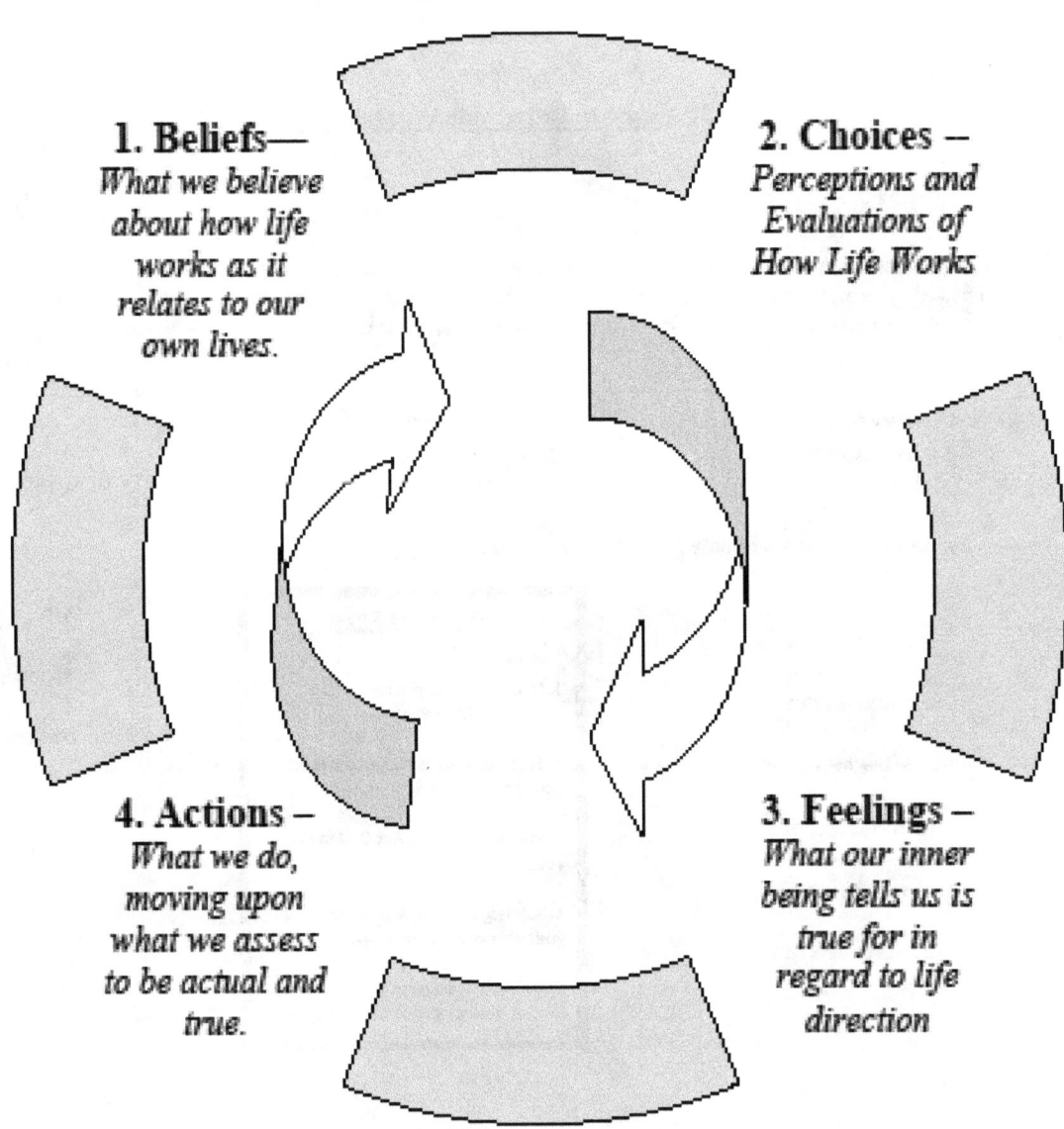

1. Beliefs— What we believe about how life works as it relates to our own lives.

2. Choices – Perceptions and Evaluations of How Life Works

3. Feelings – What our inner being tells us is true for in regard to life direction

4. Actions – What we do, moving upon what we assess to be actual and true.

Suggestions for Healthy Life Management

1. Eat healthy. Try to stay away from processed or "empty" foods. Eat live foods, or whole grains. Chicken, fish, and eggs are good sources of protein. Try to limit your intake of red meats and fats.

2. Be kind to yourself. Check for the weight you should carry on your bond structure, in order to be healthy, and try to lose the extra pounds, for the sake of your heart and knees.

3. Don't drive yourself. Take a vitamin supplement each day. Eat nuts for snacks – raw almonds or mixed nuts are good suggestions.

4. If you smoke; stop. If you drink hard alcohol; stop. Multiple and varied studies show that both of these practices will shorten your life.

5. Floss your teeth.

6. Get into a small community where you can connect and relate to others. (A class, a church, a support group, etc.)

7. Don't be afraid to say, "I don't know."

8. Learn how to apologize completely. Say, "I'm sorry. I was wrong. Would you please forgive me?"

9. How many pounds do you weigh? Cut that number in half, and drink at least that many ounces of water each day. For example, someone who weighs 120 pounds would need to drink at least 60 ounces of water each day. If you struggle with migraines, or gastric issues, more water is best.

10. Get a massage on a regular basis. 6-8 weeks between visits is recommended.

11. Get a thorough health screening. Complete all the doctor's instructions... Follow through.

12. If you live alone, take a class to keep your mind active.

13. If you don't work, volunteer at church or at a hospital to keep yourself from losing touch with the outside world.

14. Make an intentional decision to become the most positive and enthusiastic person you know. Find something good in every situation you find yourself in, and talk about that instead of the negatives you observe.

15. Take a walk every day, even when it's cold. Utilize that time to pray and connect with God's heart.

Just Take A Minute
When Fear is up to its worst, try one of these
suggestions to help your world become just a little larger.

1. Stop and look at the situation are you in the middle of. Think about it. Find the one good thing in the midst of it, and hold on to that.

2. Buy a joke book, and read at least one page of humor before you go to bed, and while you are in the bathroom each day.

3. Buy the paper, or a Reader's digest, and read the funnies.

4. Subscribe to a weekly joke email service (they're usually free).

5. Let yourself laugh out loud, without worrying about what people think about your laugh.

6. Rent some classic comedy: old black and white movies (The Marx Brothers, Oliver and Hardy, The Three Stooges).

7. Ask someone in your family to relate funny stories from their childhood.

8. Play hopscotch; by yourself or with someone much younger than you.

9. **Learn to laugh at yourself – and lighten up.** Laughing makes you a happier, healthier person. So, take the embarrassing or stupid things you do throughout the day and turn them into something positive!

10. (From USA today) When the stress of the war in Iraq becomes too severe, the Pentagon has a suggestion for military families: Learn how to laugh.

　　With help from the Pentagon's chief laughter instructor, families of National Guard members are *learning to walk like a penguin, laugh like a lion and blurt "ha, ha, hee, hee and ho, ho."*

　　No joke. "I laugh every chance I get," says the instructor, retired Army colonel James "Scotty" Scott. "That's why I'm blessed to be at the Pentagon, where we definitely need a lot of laughter in our lives."

　　Scott, is certified as a laughter training specialist by the Ohio-based World Laughter Tour, a group that promotes mirth as medicine. It touts scientific research that suggests chuckling can boost the body's immune system and decrease stress hormones.

Section Six

The Bible on Fear

Psalm 23:4   Even though I walk through the valley of the shadow of death, I will fear no evil, for you are with me; your rod and your staff, they comfort me.

Psalm 27:1   The Lord is my light and my salvation-- whom shall I fear? The LORD is the stronghold of my life-- of whom shall I be afraid?

Psalm 103:17   From everlasting to everlasting, the Lord's love is with those who fear Him, and his righteousness is with their children's children.

Psalm 115:11   You who fear Him, trust in the Lord – He is their help and shield.

Psalm 118:6   The Lord is with me; I will not be afraid. What can man do to me?

II Timothy 1:7   For God did not give us a spirit of timidity, but of power, of love and of a sound mind (self-discipline).

Psalm 122:1   Praise the Lord. Blessed is the man who fears the Lord; who finds great delight in His commands.

Deuteronomy 13:6   Be strong and courageous. Do not be afraid or terrified because of them, for the Lord your God goes with you: He will never leave you or forsake you.

Isaiah 41:10   So do not fear, for I am with you; do not be dismayed, for I am your God. I will strengthen you and help you; I will uphold you with my righteous right hand.

Isaiah 41:13   For I am the LORD, your God, who takes hold of your right hand and says to you, Do not fear; I will help you.

Isaiah 54:4   Do not be afraid; you will not suffer shame. Do not fear disgrace; you will not be humiliated. You will forget the shame of your youth and remember no more the reproach of your widowhood.

Psalm 56:3-4   When I am afraid, I will trust in you. In God, whose word I praise, in God I trust; I will not be afraid. What can mortal man do to me?

Matthew 10:28   Do not be afraid of those who kill the body but cannot kill the soul. Rather, be afraid of the One who can destroy both soul and body in hell.

Romans 8:15   For you did not receive a spirit that makes you a slave again to fear, but you received the Spirit of sonship. And by him we cry, ""Abba," Father."

1 Corinthians 16:13   Be on your guard; stand firm in the faith; be men of courage; be strong.

Hebrews 13:5-6   Keep your lives free from the love of money and be content with what you have, because God has said, "Never will I leave you; never will I forsake you." So we say with confidence, "The Lord is my helper; I will not be afraid. What can man do to me?"

1 Peter 3:13-14   Who is going to harm you if you are eager to do good? But even if you should suffer for what is right, you are blessed. "Do not fear what they fear; do not be frightened."

1 John 4:18   There is no fear in love. But perfect love drives out fear, because fear has to do with punishment. The one who fears is not made perfect in love.

Proverbs 12:25   An anxious heart weighs a man down, but a kind word cheers him up.

Psalm 34:4   I sought the LORD, and he heard me, and delivered me from all my fears.

Philippians 4:6-7   Do not be anxious about anything, but in everything, by prayer and petition, with thanksgiving, present your requests to God. And the peace of God, which transcends all understanding, will guard your hearts and your minds in Christ Jesus.

I Peter 5:6-7   Humble yourselves, therefore, under God's mighty hand, that he may lift you up in due time. Cast all your anxiety on him because he cares for you"

Luke 12:22-26   Then Jesus said to his disciples: 'Therefore I tell you, do not worry about your life, what you will eat; or about your body, what you will wear. Life is more than food, and the body more than clothes. Consider the ravens: They do not sow or reap, they have no storeroom or barn; yet God feeds them. And how much more valuable you are than birds! Who of you by worrying can add a single hour to his life? Since you cannot do this very little thing, why do you worry about the rest?' (Also see Matthew 6:25-34)

Psalm 42:5   Why are you downcast, O my soul? Why so disturbed within me? Put your hope in God, for I will yet praise him, my Savior and my God.

Proverbs 3:5-8   Trust in the LORD with all your heart and lean not on your own understanding; in all your ways acknowledge him, and he will make your paths straight. Do not be wise in your own eyes; fear the LORD and shun evil. This will bring health to your body and nourishment to your bones".

Romans 8:26-28   ...the Spirit helps us in our weakness. We do not know what we ought to pray for, but the Spirit himself intercedes for us with groans that words cannot express. And he who searches our hearts knows the mind of the Spirit, because the Spirit intercedes for the saints in accordance with God's will. And we know that in all things God works for the good of those who love him, who have been called according to his purpose.

Philippians 4:19   And my God will meet all your needs according to his glorious riches in Christ Jesus.

Hebrews 13:6   So we say with confidence, 'The Lord is my helper; I will not be afraid. What can man do to me?'

Psalm 131:1 ...put your hope in the LORD both now and forevermore."

Matthew 6:27-29   Can all your worries add a single moment to your life? And why worry about your clothing? Look at the lilies of the field and how they grow. They don't work or make their clothing, yet Solomon in all his glory was not dressed as beautifully as they are.

Matthew 6:30 And if God cares so wonderfully for wildflowers that are here today and thrown into the fire tomorrow, he will certainly care for you. Why do you have so little faith?

Section Seven

Scriptural Prayer and Supportive Materials.

To Overcome Fear

*"There is no fear in love; but perfect love casts out fear;
because fear has torment. He that fears is not made perfect in love."
I John 4:18*

When fear is present in a person's life, it is an indication of an area where the love of Father God has not been fully received and applied. The unconditional love and acceptance of God is the only thing, which can remove fear from the human heart.

Fear cannot be reasoned with --it must be confronted and commanded to leave with the Word of God and prayer.

It will help to pray in this manner:

Father God, I confess my fear to you. It is my choice to confront my fear with your Word and to command it to go from my life in the name of Jesus Christ, my Savior.

Lord, I confess that your Word says that you have not given me a spirit of fear, but of power, love and a sound mind. You have not given me a spirit of bondage, but you have adopted me and made me your own child. You have promised that no evil will befall me, and no plague will come near my dwelling place. You have given your angels charge of me, to keep me in all of my ways. You desire to be my confidence, and to keep my foot from being taken. You will keep me from oppression and terror, and establish me in righteousness.

I confess that you are my helper. You are my light and my salvation. You are the strength of my life. You are the strength of my heart, and I choose to put my hope in You.

Father, I know that nothing can separate me from Your love for me. Not tribulation, or distress, or persecution, of famine, or need, or peril, or violence. You have made me to be a conqueror over all of these things. You always love me. In every area, in every situation, you love me, without change. Nothing can separate me from your love --not death, not life, not angels, not demonic principalities, no power on earth, nothing in this present life, or in the life to come. Nothing can separate me from your love for me. You are always with me, even until the end of the earth. When I pass through waters, I will not be overwhelmed.

When I pass through rivers, they will not sweep over me. When I pass through fire, I will not be burned, for you are my Savior.

You are with me, so I will not be dismayed. You are my God and you have promised to help me, strengthen me, and uphold me with your righteous right hand. You preserve me from trouble and sing songs of deliverance over my life. You deliver me from all of my fears. I will trust in you. You are my refuge and fortress, and you will come with a vengeance, and You will save me. You have promised to contend with those that contend with me, and to save my children. You have promised that no weapon formed against me will prosper, and every tongue that rises up against me will be condemned. You have promised to strengthen me by Your Spirit with might in the inner man.

I plead the covering of the Blood of the Lamb over my soul. Fear, you have no authority in speak into my life, or to influence me. I will stand firm and see the deliverance the Lord has for me. I do not even have to fight this battle, for the battle is not mine, but it belongs to God. You have been defeated by the death of the Son of God, and I will not give you place any longer.

Isaiah 41:10-13	Romans 8:15	Isaiah 43:1-3	Isaiah 41:10
Philippians 1:28	Psalm 27:1	Psalm 91:1,4-7,10-11	Isaiah 54:14
Hebrews 13:6	Psalm 31:24	Deuteronomy 31:6-8	Proverbs 3:25-26
Exodus 14:13	Romans 8:29,31,35-39		II Chronicles 20:15
II Timothy 1:1	Isaiah 12:2	Psalm 21:1,3	

To Overcome Prejudice and Hatred

"(He) hath made of one blood all nations of men
for to dwell on all the face of the earth,
and hath determined the times before appointed,
and the bounds of their habitation." Acts 17:26

Hatred and prejudice are usually passed down through generational sin, through involvement of a family member in the Klan, civil rights demonstrations and protests, or some type of civil war, or even unkind slurs and prejudicial statements heard and laughed at within intimate family gatherings.

The love of God has no boundaries, or degrees, when it comes to color, race, or station. We are called to express that kind of love without reserve. God is not a respecter of persons. This aspect of His character is addressed pointedly in Scripture. Our heavenly Father does not express favoritism. He blesses righteousness, wherever and whenever a heart is focused upon Him.

Prejudice and hatred must be faced squarely and honestly, with assessment of willful actions and subconscious reactions. These qualities are weak points in a person's spiritual life, when demonic influence can bring bondage in the areas of anger, rage and violence; control, and fear. When the light of the Word is shone on an area, it can be painful to look at, but the Father is faithful to set the heart free.

It will help to pray in this manner:

Father God, I acknowledge You as my Heavenly Father and Creator. You have created all men on the face of the earth with one blood, and You have provided the covering of one Blood for our cleansing and wholeness. I confess to you my battle with prejudice and hatred. Hatred has blinded my eyes to the troth of your unconditional love and acceptance for all people. When I have acted out of rejection, in rejecting them, I have rejected You. Please forgive me for my hardness of heart. Remove this heart of stone, and replace it with a heart of flesh. I choose to have an open, teachable, and loving heart.

Father God, Your Word declares that those who hate your people bring a curse upon themselves, and are clothed with shame and are desolate. I cut off the life of every curse and desolation I have brought upon my own life through my hatred and prejudice in the name of Jesus Christ. Your Word declares that those who hate love death.
I cut off every attachment I have opened for my soul to the spirit of death in the name of Jesus Christ.

Father God, I repent and renounce all instances of prejudice and hatred in my family background. I cut off that influence from my spiritual and emotional life, and I break the power of that heritage in my life. I will not be ruled by hatred. I will not allow prejudice to blind my vision and understanding.

It is my choice to recognize that Satan is the author of hatred and prejudice. I hate him with a perfect hatred, and I count him as my enemy, rather than counting flesh and blood as my enemy.

I plead the blood of the Lamb over my soul. Hatred, I remove every legal right you have to speak into my life. Prejudice, you have lost your place of influence. I will stand firm and see the deliverance the Lord Jesus has for me. I do not even have to fight this battle, for the battle is not mine, but it belongs to God. You have been defeated by the death and resurrection of the Son of God, and I will not give you place any longer. I choose to be free.

Psalm 109:3	Leviticus 19:17	Psalm 139:22	Proverbs 10:18
Psalm 34:21	Galatians 5:20	Luke 6:22	Deuteronomy 30:7
Job 8:22	II Chronicles 19:7	Proverbs 1:2	Job 34:19
Deut. 10:17	Deuteronomy 16:1	Romans 2:9-10	Psalm 109:5
Proverbs 24:23	Acts 10:34	Proverbs 26:26	Romans 2:11

To Overcome Pride (specifically, the Spirit of Contention and Perfectionism

"The fear of the Lord is to hate evil, pride, and arrogance." Proverbs 8:13

Pride is the basis of every sin. It is the expression of Satan's nature, vented through the flesh. It is the assertion of "rights", and the desire to prove oneself to be right, at whatever cost. It is the root of self-sufficiency and independence. Its tendency is to set standards and expect others to measure up to them, without first seeking God for his direction and plan. It is trusting in one's own abilities and strengths, and then expecting a blessing for a "good" idea.

Pride must be confronted daily in the human soul. If given any ground, the deceit of pride will gain ground in every area and render the believer useless and ineffective in prayer and
in service.

Signs of Pride:

1. No answer to prayer when in need (John 35:12)
2. A persecution (disregard) for the poor. (Psalm 10:2)
3. Cursing and lying. (Psalm 59:12)
4. Violence. (Psalm 73:6)
5. Shame. (Proverbs 11:2)
6. Contention. (Proverbs 13:10)
7. Deception. (Jeremiah 49:16, Obadiah 3)

It will help to pray in this manner:

Father God, I am confronted by my own willful desires to do things my way. I confess to you the pride within my own heart. I have thought more highly of myself than I ought to think. I have allowed myself to have contentious thoughts -- thoughts which argue against those who you have placed in my life as authority figures. I repent for the foolish words of my mouth, which have exalted my own opinions and attitudes, but have resisted teachability.

Your Word says that you hate even a proud look. Please be the lifter of my head and the light of my countenance. I renounce every door I have opened within my soul for pride to operate and gain influence. The wicked, through pride, will not seek after You, but Lord, I desire to seek you. Please reveal and root out every prideful thing within me. I will not walk with the foot of pride, or allow pride to provoke me to anger. I cut off that influence in Jesus' name. I humble myself before You, Lord.

I humble myself before You, Lord. Remove all pride and selfish ambition from me.
I repent and renounce the influences of flattery in my life. Father, please forgive me for the times I have listened to man's flattery and allowed it to shape the image of who you desire me to be. I only want to be what you want me to be. I repent and renounce every flattering word in the name of Jesus.

I repent and renounce every lie and deception I have practiced because of the influence of pride. With the fear of the Lord comes wisdom, but the fool is proud. It is my desire to be filled with the fear of the Lord; that I will not fall into the trap of Pride again. I cut off the chains of pride with the Blood of the Lamb of God.

It is my choice to cut off from my life a proud look, a haughty attitude, a lying tongue, and the sowing of discord among the brethren. I know and understand that you hate these things. I choose to show mercy and unconditional love to all I come in contact with. I choose to be a peace-maker, and be called a son of God.

It is my choice to clothe myself with humility as with a garment, and to regard Your workings in me as wondrous and miraculous. No longer will look for what I consider myself to have earned. I choose to wait upon You, Lord, for your purposes and plans for my life. I cast down every vain imagination, which exalts itself against the knowledge of God in my life. I will not look to myself, and my own abilities for answers from this time forward.

Pride, I will not serve to express you any longer. I cut off every bud and seed of pride from growing in my life and soul. I belong to the Lord God of Hosts, and' I choose to be under His authority. I will not seek to be my own authority. The Blood of the Lamb of God is against you, and is applied to the door of my life. You have no authority to speak to me, because I choose to remove every legal right I have given you to deal in my life. You cannot speak into my life, or influence me, because my hope is in the Lord Jesus Christ and His work upon the Cross for me. I stand in the accomplished work of the Blood of Jesus. I will not give you place any longer.

Psalm 36:11	Psalm 59:12	Psalm 73:6	Proverbs 8:13
Proverbs 13:10	Proverbs 14:3	Proverbs 16:18	Ezekiel 7:10
Daniel 5:20	Mark 7:22	I John 2:16	Psalm 4:6
Psalm 12:3	Psalm 40:4	Psalm 123:4	Proverbs 6:16-17
Proverbs 15:25	Proverbs 16:5	Proverbs 21:4	Proverbs 28:25

How to Strengthen Your Will to Choose God's Way

The following are suggestions for you to follow when you find your will is weak to obey the Spirit of the Lord, or authority figures He has placed in your life. Anyone suggestion will help to strengthen your will. As you find yourself becoming stronger in obedience, it is a good idea to add more steps, until all have been completed.

The **minimum** time spent on each of these steps should be 30 days.

~~~~~~~~~~~~~~~~~~~~~~~~~~~~~~

1. Choose and commit to pray in the Spirit for 1 hour a day. (Do not plan to do this all at once. Pray in 12 increments of 5 minutes, or 6 increments of 10 minutes at regular times each day.) It works well to set a timer, so that you do not short yourself on the edifying benefit of prayer.

2. Choose and commit to read the Word of God. Read 5-15 verses **out loud** to yourself on a daily basis. Read the same portion of scripture 3 times through. Here are some recommended sections, which will shine the Father's light on your will.

Ephesians 2:1-10	Ephesians 4:30-32
Colossians 3:1-10	John 14:23-30
Colossians 3:5-11	Revelation 3:14-22
II Corinthians 3:1-18	Luke 6:46-48
Ephesians 4:14-22	Ephesians 5:1-12
Colossians 2:6-10	Colossians 1:9-14
I Thessalonians 5:8-23	II Corinthians 4:1-7
John 15:1-11	

3. Choose and commit to memorizing the Word of God, with references. Quote the scriptures you have memorized to those who are walking your through the process of strengthening your will. Here are some suggested verses:

John 4:34	John 6:38
Matthew 26:41	Matthew 7:13-14

4. Choose and commit to worship the Father for a specific amount of undistracted, private time -just you and God. Set 3 minutes as a beginning place. This should be stretched into a 15-minute segment as your will progresses in obedience. If need be, set a timer to help you. Sing worship songs, and focus on the Father's love for you.

5. Choose and commit to do a word study from the Word of God on Obedience.

6. Choose and commit to fast 2 meals in one day, and read the Word instead of eating. Read Psalm 23 through Psalm 34 out loud to yourself each time you do so. This should be done once a month to begin with, and then progressively brought into a weekly practice.

7. On a piece of paper, make 2 columns. Label the columns, "Things which strengthen my will to obey", and "Things which weaken my will to obey." Look up the following scriptures and fill in the categories you find.

I Peter 3:21	I Timothy 4:2	Titus 1:5
I Timothy 1:9	Romans 13:5	Romans 6:16
Romans 8:7	Galatians 3:1	Matthew 7:21
I Corinthians 8:12	Romans 2:15	James 3:18
Romans 2:6-10	Proverbs 6:12-15	Joshua 24:24
Acts 5:32	Galatians 5:7	Matthew 7:24-27
Proverbs 1:28-31	Matthew 24:12	Titus 3:1
Hebrews 13:17	Hebrews 12:9	Nehemiah 9:17
Romans 2:8	John 14:15	I Chronicles 12:33

8. Rewrite the following scriptures, and substitute personal and impersonal pronouns with your own first name, and "his/him or hers/her", etc. Then commit yourself to memorize each one.

Romans 8:15	Isaiah 54:14,15, and 17	Deuteronomy 31:8
I John 4:4	Isaiah 43:1-3	Luke 10:19
Isaiah 41:10	II Timothy 4:18	Psalm 23
Isaiah 42:16	Philippians 1:6	Lamentations 3:22
II Thessalonians 3:3	Isaiah 59:11	Ezekiel 34:16
Jeremiah 29:11	Hebrews 13:5	Psalm 120:7
I Corinthians 10:13	I Corinthians 1:5	Acts 2:39

9. Keep a journal of the scriptures and truths, which have become real to your own heart. When pain comes close to the surface these things will encourage your heart and help you.

10. When your emotions rise up, and try to control your actions and responses, by using painful memories and experiences, take the time to write them down. Then, find an accountability friend (someone who you can trust to keep things confidential and whose love you are secure with), to pray through each instance with. It is also a good idea to take communion, and apply the blood of Jesus specifically to each area in question.

Practical Strategies to Lower Fear Attacks When They Occur:

1. Slow down your breathing. Try to focus on resting your mind. Allow the peace of God to rule your heart and mind. (Colossians 3:15-16)

2. Read the Word of God out loud, especially passages that are directly addressed to the subject of fear and anxiety. Receive the comfort of the Holy Spirit as you contemplate these Scriptures.

3. Pray. Sing worship songs. Give thanks for the Lord's direction and help in your life to this point. Remember that He has never failed you, and has promised to always be with you. He is your Helper.

4. Find a spot with no electronic gadgets, no clocks, no cell phones. Stay there for 30 minutes. Allow your heart to re-connect with the Lord. Pray, and then listen.

5. Picture a quiet lake, or imagine walking on the beach.

6. Consider: The intelligence with which Father has created the universe. *Fact: a single human cell measuring 1/1,000 of an inch across, contains instructions within its DNA that would fill 1,000 books of 600 pages each.* Take time to contemplate, and meditate upon your own life's intrinsic value in the scheme of such an intricate design.

7. Turn on slow, quiet music. Let go of your stress.

8. Surrender areas of resistance and anger to the Holy Spirit. Allow your year to be patient with the speed of your growth and development. Maturity cannot be rushed. It takes lessons, and it takes time.

9. Darken your environment, sit in a chair with your eyes closed for 2 minutes.

10. Think of a happy memory, and try to mentally place yourself in that situation once again.

11. Take time to journal, or if possible, seek connection and reassurance from a friend.

12. Go for a walk.

13. Share time with another person whom you trust, and talk about your fears.

14. Hold and stroke a pet, allowing your heart to be comforted. If you don't have a pet, sometimes it can be useful to hold a soft, stuffed animal.

Steps To Begin the Journey Out Of The Fear Trap

Step One — *Utilizing the assessment materials provided in this packet, step back and take an objective look at you are handling the perceived stressors in your life. What recurring theme do you see in these assessments? What do you worry about most? Is something constantly on your mind? What is your first thought in the morning? Is there anything in particular that causes you to experience sadness or depression? Take a few moments for several days in a row, and journal (write down) your observations.*

Step Two — *Take time to evaluate the nutrition and exercise levels in your life. Are you taking care of the temple the Lord has given you? Limit your caffeine, nicotine and alcohol intake. Begin by providing your body with the minimum of a multiple daily vitamin. Begin to get enough sleep, and exercise regularly.*

Step Three — *Take a look at your personality. Are you addicted to adrenaline? Do you thrive on a fast lifestyle, or hurried lifestyle? For example, if you are a Type A, you will tend to be more prone to stress and anxiety – (interruptive, competitive, over-plan each day, low tolerance of frustration, don't wait well, deep sense of justice, sleeps less than 7 hours nightly, prone to high stress, strong sense of time urgency, tendency to deal with anger at times—You will have to work harder at managing your stress and anxiety levels.)*

If you are a Type B, you will find yourself not having the same difficulties with stress as a Type A, but your anxiety levels could be linked to other issues. Type B personalities are lower in stress, move slower, more patient and easy-going, more tolerant, and sleep longer, 9-10 hours per night.

Step Four — *Become aware of how much adrenaline you are pumping and what type of activities increase your adrenaline.*

Step Five — *When anxiety arises, stop. Slow down your breathing rate. Ask yourself: "Is this an emergency?" "Is this worth dying for?" Talk to yourself objectively. Lower your adrenaline, by focusing on relaxing.*

Step Six — *Begin to plan ahead for high demand moments. Try to plan your time and schedule efficiently and realistically. Cut back on extra activities that bring on stress. Begin to restrict demands upon yourself, and allow yourself to draw boundaries for perceived demands. Allow yourself to rest regularly, and after high stress situations.*

Step Seven   *Make a conscious choice to open your heart to the Spirit of God. Get into a solid community group of believers, and set your goals to establish relationships in which you establish healthy understandings of how life works. Make a decision to admit the places in your life where you have resisted bonding with others, and with God, especially those places in your heart that you are afraid to talk about.*

Step Eight   *Choose to maintain relationships, even when difficult times come. Choose not to return to the places of darkness and fear that used to be your safe place.*

Step Nine   *Keep your heart focused on establishing and maintaining a lifestyle of worship. Memorize what the Word of God says about fear, and apply those promises to your life each day, doing your best to walk away from fear, unlearning your fears, and re-learning the Lord's promises.*

Step Ten   *Keep your heart open and accountable. Purpose to receive the love of God, and give away that love as well.*

Lies That Tie Us To Oppression

The Lie: "God expects me to do things perfectly."

    The Truth: Galatians 3:3
                  II Cor. 12:9
                  Psalm 18:32

The Lie: "I need to keep a perfect environment."
    The Truth: II Samuel 22:33

The Lie: "I must please everyone; I must keep everyone happy."
    The Truth: Colossians 2:6-8

The Lie: "I need everyone's approval."
    The Truth: Galatians 1:10

The Lie: "I need to be like everyone else in order to be right."
    The Truth: II Corinthians 10:12

The Lie: "I must defend myself, or no one will..."
    The Truth: Psalm 31:15
                  Psalm 91:1-3
                  Psalm 119:114

The Lie: "I must create a place for myself."
    The Truth: Proverbs 18:16

The Lie: "Close relationships with other people are dangerous."
    The Truth: Eccl. 4:9-12
                  Proverbs 27:9-10;
                  Proverbs 18:24

The Lie: "Being vulnerable is unsafe. I can't tell anyone my struggles."

    The Truth: James 5:16
                  Eph. 4:13-15

The Lie: "I am on the outside. I don't belong."

    The Truth: Ephesians 1:3-12

The Lie: "I must earn my place."

    The Truth: II Timothy 1:9
                  Titus 3:5-7

The Lie: "What I do determines my worth."

    The Truth: Matt. 10:26-31
                  Luke 12:6-7
                  Ephesians 2:8-10
                  Psalm 139:14-18

The Lie: "God does not want to talk to me."
    The Truth: John 16:12-15

The Lie: "I must take the blame for there to be peace in my relationships."

    The Truth: Galatians 6:5

The Lie: "Love and sexual expression are the same thing..."

    The Truth: I Thess. 4:3-8
                  I Corinthians 13

The Lie: "Conflict is always bad."

    The Truth: Ephesians 6:12

The Lie: "I can't trust anyone else with my heart, and my inner desires."

    The Truth: Ephesians 5:21
                  I Cor. 13:4-7

The Lie: "I must make my own way."

    The Truth: I Peter 3:8-9

The Lie: "Respect and fear are the same thing. I must fear authority."
    The Truth: II Timothy 1:7
                  Romans 8:15-17

The Lie: "I must protect my own interests to be heard, and to be safe."
    The Truth: Philippians 2:3-4
                  I Peter 4:8-11

The Lie: "I must be in control to be heard and to be safe."
    The Truth: Deut. 30:6

© atg, dcg

Suggested Reading List – Fear Issues

1. **Breaking Intimidation: Say "No" Without Feeling Guilty. Be Secure without the Approval of Man** by John Bevere. (ISBN: 978-1591858812) Published by Charisma House; revised edition, 2005. 224 pages.

2. **Beyond Negative Thinking: Breaking The Cycle Of Depressing And Anxious Thoughts** by Joseph T. Martorano and John P. Kildahl (ISBN:978-0738206172) Published by Perseus Publishing, 2001. 304 pages

3. **The Anxiety Cure** by Dr. Archibald D. Hart, (ISBN: 978-0849942969) Published by Thomas Nelson Publishers, 2001. 263 pages

4. **Hurt People Hurt People: Hope and Healing for Yourself and Your Relationships Paperback** by Dr. Sandra D. Wilson, (ISBN: 978-1572930162) Published by Discovery House Publishers. 265 pages.

5. **Effective Biblical Counseling: A Model for Helping Caring Christians Become Capable Counselors** by Larry Crabb, (ISBN: 978-0310225706) Published by Zondervan Publishing House, 1977. 212 pages

6. **Why Does He Do That? Inside the Minds of Angry and Controlling Men by Lundy Bancroft.** (ISBN 978-0425191651) Published by Berkley Books, Reprint edition, 2003. 432 pages

More from Awakened to Grow…

Be sure to complete your set of ATG's handbooks from **A Christian Counselor's Primer On…** series. Titles include Depression, Communication, Fear and Anxiety, Processing Grief, and many more! Each reference tool contains charts and assessments for personal discovery and development. Recorded teaching sessions are available for each handbook. Just contact us through our website! Handbooks vary in length and are priced at $20 each. *(Published, 2014)*

Elements of Identity Formation – Outlines and charts help the student understand the process of emotional and spiritual identity formation. Especially helpful for all those who struggle with understanding how to experience the love of God on a personal level. Recorded teaching sessions are available for each handbook. Just contact us through our website! *Workbook is available on amazon.com and lulu.com*

journey – a novel; The real story of a girl called "Magdalene." A compelling weaving of historical and Biblical events, this painstakingly researched account of the life of Mary Magdalene will surprise you in how it relates to our present culture and your own personal history. 504 pages *(2nd edition)* $33.50 (MSRP) (Published, 2009 & 2014) *Available at amazon.com and/or lulu.com*

Secrets for Relational Living -- For every person who wants to experience healthy relationships! This 8 session class can be studied individually or with a group. Video sessions of the teachings are available through our website. Especially helpful for all those who feel inwardly insecure in successfully communicating and relating to others.
Available on amazon.com and lulu.com

The Chronicles of Hausse – Book One; The Trouble with Dragons -- An allegorical adventure, set in the mystical land of Hausse; where Lightbearers and Demons can be seen and danger lurks around every corner! Written to explain the spiritual realm to middle school and high school aged students, this book has received rave reviews from readers from 8 to 80! 368 pages $22.00 (MSRP) (Published, 2012) *Available at amazon.com and/or lulu.com*

For a more complete listing, please check out our listings on Amazon.com and lulu.com. Please also see our worship/music resources on iTunes.

www.ingramcontent.com/pod-product-compliance
Lightning Source LLC
Chambersburg PA
CBHW080347170426
43194CB00014B/2710